Knowing What It Takes:

A Parent's Guide to College Athletics Eligibility

Toya White

Knowing What It Takes

A Parent's Guide to College Athletics Eligibility

Inspire Athletics Consulting Group, Inc.

www.inspireathleticscg.org

ISBN-13: 978-0692697481

ISBN- 10: 0692697489

Published By: Learn2Inspire

Printed in the United States of America

Dedication

This book is dedicated to my brother, Taiwan Lamar White, (4/2/83-3/28/15) may you rest in peace. Thank you for teaching me to always live life, have fun, and keep it moving no matter what. You were simply amazing and you are truly missed. To my reasons for being, Travonte, Camari, and Braylen. I love each of you in ways you will never know. You all are the reason I live. To my goddaughter Curtresse, I have watched you grow into such a beautiful young lady. Very proud to be a part of your life, love you. To my mother, Stephanie, thank you for always listening to me and being there at a moment's notice. You are the epitome of a mother and I strive to be like you daily. To my godfather Moses, I love you more than I say, thank you for being there in ways I may have not gotten a chance to experience. To my brother Tavin, thank you for always being here for me, I can count on my hands the time I have heard no from you, I appreciate you. To my sister-in-law, Quinnett, thank you for assuming a role you didn't have to play, but you did to help me and for that I am forever indebted to you and appreciate you more than you can ever imagine, you are indeed an angel, love you. To my brother Trent, thank you for always giving me that encouragement I needed to see things in a different way, you are truly a blessing and I adore you. To my brother Travis, thank you for always listening and helping me when I need you most, I appreciate you. To my one and only sister, Taffy, I have enjoyed watching you grow into the woman you are today, love you dearly. To my stepfather, Leon, thank you for accepting us all and making my mom happy, you are amazing for being that person for her, love you. To my dad, Ray, thank you for helping me with my lesson on forgiveness and seeing the big picture. To my nephews and nieces, I love each of you. Always do your best no matter what it is you do, respect yourself and others, and make decisions that you are comfortable with. Each of you mean the world to me and I value each of you. If it wasn't for you, there would be no me. I appreciate each of you. I hope you enjoy this. Thank you. God bless.

Acknowledgements

First all, giving honor to God, from whom all my blessing flow. Thankful for the opportunity to write and to help others. The journey of writing has been an amazing one for me. The time put in has been well worth it. I am grateful for everyone that has assisted me in any way. With that being said, I would like to take time to acknowledge the ones who helped make my vision a reality. I appreciate each of you for your support.

Christian Radford, my sister and my editor. You never complained as I sent you chapter after chapter to read and edit. Thank you for everything. Love you.

George Frazier, my coworker and friend, my second brain on this journey. Thank you for your support and believing in me. You never hesitated when I came to you from the start with my idea. You have made this process so much easier. Thank you.

Royce Dickerson, my friend and graphic designer. Thank you for always coming to my rescue at a moment's notice. You will always be on my team. Love you.

To all my coach friends and associates, thank you for your time spent answering questions, listening to me, reading some of the information, and overall support. I appreciate each of you.

Corry Black- Director at CBlackhoops.com & JucoReport.com- Talent Evaluator, Columbus, GA

Johnny White- Head Football Coach- Douglas County High School-Douglasville, GA

Darius Hodge- Head Boys Basketball Coach- Hiram High School-Hiram, GA

Terrone Owens- Assistant Head Football Coach/Offensive Coordinator-Lamar County High School- Barnesville, GA

Patrice Bryant- Head Girls Basketball Coach- Langston Hughes High School- Fairburn, GA

Myron Terry- Head Football Coach- New Manchester High School-Douglasville, GA

Anthony Hickey- Head Girls Basketball Coach- Christian County High School- Hopkinsville, KY

Travis Smith- Assistant Head Football Coach/Offensive Coordinator-Douglas County High School-Douglasville, GA

Tony Dews- Assistant Coach/ Wide Receivers- The University of Arizona-Tucson, AZ

Craig Agee- Assistant Coach/Wide Receivers- Tuskegee University - Tuskegee, AL

Bruce Capers- Men's Basketball Head Coach- Gordon State College-Barnesville, GA

Table of Contents

About the Author

Toya White is a native of Hopkinsville, Kentucky where she grew up with four brothers and one sister. She was raised by her mother and her grandmother. She graduated from Christian County High School there in Hopkinsville, KY. Toya went on to live in Canton, OH where she attended Stark State College and receive her Associates Degree in Computer Applications. She went on to attend University of Phoenix, where she received her Bachelor of Science Degree in Business Management and her Masters of Business Administration.

After living in Ohio for several years, Toya decided to move back South, she ended in Atlanta, Georgia. It was here that she found her love for education and working with young adults. She received her teaching certificate from The University of Georgia and went on to receive her Educational Specialist Degree from Nova Southeastern. She has been in the high school setting for the past 9 years as an educator. She finds joy in assisting high school student with staying on track and reaching their goals in the classroom and in life. She currently serves as a Career Technical Coordinator in the high school setting daily assisting students with their aspirations for the next level of life after graduating high school.

She also runs a non-profit organization, Inspire Athletics Consulting, where she assist student-athletes with grades, test prep, and staying on track for graduation as well as NCAA eligibility. (www.inspireathleticscg.org)

Toya currently resides in Atlanta, Georgia with her three beautiful children, Travonte (17), Camari (7), and Braylen (4). The experiences of motherhood and being involved in sports with her children, mainly her oldest, has taught her so much. Taking the education aspect and connecting it with the athletic aspect for a student-athletes is what Toya lives for. She formed her non-profit organization, Inspire Athletic Consulting Group, in 2015 to educate parents and student-athletes on the importance of academics and athletics and how they must work together in order for a student-athletes to be all around successful. Toya continues to speak with parents and athletes and give them the tools that help student-athletes succeed academically so they can soar athletically.

Introduction

I am that parent that said my son will be ready when it comes to college, and I was going to do what it took to make sure he is successful. My son has always played sports; baseball, football, and basketball all at once. My days were long during the season and the summers, but I didn't mind because I wanted to foster that growth and interest he had in sports. Being a single mother, I wanted to keep him out of trouble, keep him active, and get him involved with good people. Sports were a way to do just that. As time passed by, my son began to take on a special interest in basketball above all other sports. He lived and breathed basketball, playing it year round. I was always on the go, meeting other parents just like me, meeting coaches, and seeing new places. I loved it just as much as he did.

Basketball was going great. I watched my son play on the Varsity team beginning his freshman year, and then start Varsity the next three years. It was a great feeling. I knew there was more to this game and wanted to make sure he knew it as well. The things I knew did not scratch the surface on the things I learned with the relationship between academics, scholarships, types of colleges, importance of SAT/ACT test, the recruiting process, and just being overall supportive.

With all the information I obtained, I began to wonder how other parents felt and immediately I knew that I had to help out in some way. It is my hope that you, as the parent, will find the material in this book helpful in making sure your student-athlete has a successful high school career and prepared to pursue collegiate level academics and sports, should that be THEIR desire, yes THEIR desire, not yours.

Enjoy!

Academic Years

Most of the time when a child enters high school, they are just happy to be in high school. Many are not as focused on their studies as parents would like for them to be. The transition from middle to high school, can be a big adjustment and the new found freedom seems like a great privilege. The first part of freshman year is spent getting acclimated to advanced classes, lunch schedule, learning different teachers, carrying books, figuring out lockers, and then trying to play a sport. This is all done while trying to accomplish your goals. I get tired thinking about all of that as an adult, so imagine what the students deal with in the new environment. As an educator, I see it year after year; the freshman class is so excited and sometimes academics can be the last things on their little minds. For this reason alone, as parents, we have to instill the importance of academics into our children and student-athletes alike.

For a student who wants to attend college on scholarship, whether academically or athletically, each core grade matters, and will be used to calculate their overall grade point average. From the end of your student's eighth grade year, you should know what classes they will take upon registering for their freshman year. Of course, there are state graduation requirements that you have to follow, and most counselors do a good job of making sure at least the core classes are right, but it does go beyond that. With that being said, let me say, please do not solely rely on your high school counselor to be the say all, end all of your child's high school experience. You as well as your child must know what requirements are needed, and lay out the plan to get to the end successfully. Hopefully, without having to repeat any courses. During their 8th grade year, your child should know what classes are required of them their freshman year, and be preparing mentally to take on those classes. Also taking time to develop a schedule that sets aside time for studying and after school tutoring so they will not fall behind; along with the practice schedule for the particular sport your child may be involved in. I will refer to Georgia's graduation requirements because that is where I'm currently an educator in a high school setting.

A freshman's first year in high school or even college, is definitely the hardest due to the overall adjustment. It can make you or break you. It's like a newly turned 21 year old that has graduated college and is now entering into the real world. You have people you can count on to be there for you. But, you don't want to let them down so you try to figure it all out on your own, making mistakes, but trying to correct them before anyone else finds out. There will be many mistakes made during your student's freshman year of high school, but they will need to be quickly corrected if they plan to be successful. Being successful is the name of the game, so laying a solid foundation is key. Look at it as building a house. With a student's freshman year being the foundation, it has to be solid. Taking the necessary courses and making the grades are vital.

When registering for freshman year, counselors will place automatically place students in core classes. Core classes are courses that all students are required to complete before they can move on to the next grade level in their educational journey. Core classes come from the subject areas of Mathematics, Science, Social Studies, and Language Arts. These are classes that a student must take as part of their graduation requirements, and are used in the calculation of grade point averages for college purposes. As an athlete, the core classes have to be NCAA (National Collegiate Athletic Association) approved courses, which I will discuss more in depth later. The NCAA is the governing organization for all student-athletes that wish to attend a college and play a sport at that level. After being placed in core classes, the counselors will normally ask students what their interest are and select elective classes that will aid in allowing them to explore a career pathway of their choice. While elective classes are important in graduating from high school, they have no bearing on the core grade point average. However, they do impact the overall grade point average and should be taken just as seriously as an English or Mathematics class. There is an exception to the rule of the class not counting as a core class. If the specific elective appears on that NCAA approved course list that I mentioned earlier, it is considered a core course, and can be used to calculate core grade point averages for NCAA standards. It is important for your student to have some ideas of what offered electives they may be interested in such as business class, computer classes, automotive, culinary, cosmetology, JROTC program, engineering, etc. The list of career pathways (electives) varies from school to school, but having your student put in a pathway that they actually have interest in is better than just throwing them in a class to satisfy the elective credits required by the state for graduation. Oh, there is that word, credit. Let's talk about credits.

Credits are gained by successfully passing your classes. While many core classes may be a yearlong, it truly depends on the way the school is set up and how credits are given. For a school that is on semesters, your student will get a grade at the end of each semester. Once this grade is on your child's report card or transcript, it counts. There are some that may take a course over to improve the grade, but there are rules for this as well. It has to be done before their senior year in order to be used in calculation of core GPA for the NCAA requirements for student-athletes. For a freshman that is laying that foundation, passing classes has a lot of weight for a schedule that is on semesters, because they could get further behind in credits faster than a student that is on yearlong credit schedule. If a student, on a semester schedule, fails to meet passing grade then they will not receive credit for that half of the course, but they are still able to continue on for the next half of the course and pass it, if they are successful, there will be 0.5 credit earned for that course. Now, the downside to that is the 0.5 credit not met from first semester will have to be made up.

Making up a course often means going to summer school or doubling in that subject area the next year. This means they would take the first semester of the 9th grade Literature class along with 10th grade Literature to catch up. Once a student has to do this, they will have to be willing to work very hard to stay on top of it all. The ultimate goal is to get the material and pass the class the first time around so you do not fall behind and can maintain passing grades in all classes and not be stressed with more on the plate than can handle, which could be a disaster. With a student who is on a yearlong credit schedule, they may not be passing the class at the end of the first semester (before Christmas break) but when they come back from break, they have the second half of the school year to bring that grade up and pass the class to receive the credit.

Being in a situation where you have to make up courses is not good because you are missing material that will allow you to be successful in the course that succeeds the course you failed. Example: Johnny failed Algebra the first semester of his 9th grade year. Now Johnny is struggling in the second half of the class because he missed important material. The end of school year comes, and the counselor places Johnny in 10th grade level math, which is normally Geometry, along with the first semester of the Algebra he failed his 9th grade year. Now Johnny has two math classes and has to work his butt off to make the grades to pass the classes. Johnny got himself into this situation by not taking the material seriously the first time. Parents, it is important to keep up with your child's grades because they often do not say when they need help, but grades will always tell the truth. Keeping up with your child's grades has been made easy by most school systems. Parents just have to sign up for the system used to communicate grades to parents. In Georgia, most counties use what is called Infinite Campus. It is a parent portal that allows you to see grades, attendance, communicate with teachers and just be able to stay on top of academics for your student. Don't allow your child to struggle, make sure they are attending tutorial, and if needed, get them outside help to be successful. Know what credits your child needs, devise a plan, and do all that you can be see it through.

Now you have heard NCAA approved course, and probably wondering, what that means. There is a list of NCAA approved courses by school that are available for your child to take. These courses will calculate into the grade point average to determine eligibility according to NCAA requirements, which are changing as of August 2016. Most states' high school graduation requirements should align with NCAA requirements because states require more to graduate. If a child follows it, they most likely will be okay with NCAA requirements as well if appropriate grades are maintained. The most important thing to remember is making the best grade possible to receive more points towards grade point average. There are also what some schools would consider elective classes, (Psychology, Sociology, etc., and as I stated earlier, the grades received from these classes can be used as part of NCAA calculation if on the approved list. Be sure to check with the school counselor before registering your student for one of these courses. Each year counts, but it is the freshman year that carries the most weight because it sets the foundation for your student-athlete to build on. Consider 9th grade the foundation to your child's home, 10th and 11th grades are the sides to the home, with the completion coming 12th grade year, the top of it all. If the 9th grade courses are laid right, with great grades obtained, then each year that follows will be about making the grades, staying eligible and pursuing scholarships when the time comes. This will be discussed later.

The thing to take away from this section is that each academic year counts, from freshman year to the end of senior year. It will be in the best interest of your child to make the grades the first time and to stay on track. Support your child and make sure you sign up for parent portal. Most school systems invest in this as a way for parents to keep up with their child's academic progress. Attend open house, meet your child's teachers and make sure they have your contact info. Schedule parent

teachers conferences if and when needed, and even if not needed, just to

check in and let them know you are there. With all these forms of

communication in place, and with a solid foundation for your student,

freshman to senior years can be the best experience your child has ever

had. Senior year should be smooth, and the time when students are

taking the last of core classes, having fun, doing senior activities and

preparing for the next phase of life. Whether it be pursuing straight

academics or being a student-athlete at the collegiate level, it can be done

and done right with no worries if there is dedication to see it through,

great work ethic, and focus.

While I have given you the breakdown of Georgia's high school graduation

requirements, you can also find a list at back of book of other states'

graduation requirements. Please refer to Page 98.

Understanding Your Child's Ability Level

Where do I begin with this one? Can you think back to something that as a child, you said you would do as an adult, then life got in the way and you were not able to do that particular thing? I am sure we all have more than one of those stories to share. Well, please, I repeat please do not try to live your life through your child or make them do something because that is what you want them to do. As a child, of course, our kids have to listen to us and follow our rules, but as times goes on, they grow older. With this growing older, comes understanding life, and what they want to pursue post-graduation. As the parent, you are there to guide this, but this should not be your decision to make solely. Your child should be able to have a voice in their future and it be accepted by you (as long as it isn't outrageous of course). This acceptance comes with knowing your child's ability level, both academically and athletically. Let's take a look at the academic side of it first. I will always put academics first before anything.

So what do I mean by knowing your child's ability level? In school, there was always a subject that you did not like as much as another subject. Back in our times, we knew that we had to make passing grades, no matter what. We didn't even second guess not passing a test, or bringing home a report card with a failing grade on it. We were scared of our parents and we worked our butts off to make the grade and to make our parents proud. We dare not have an attitude with a teacher and definitely not at home. Today's society has given our students the idea that it is ok to not put your best foot forward and push to make the grade. Our students today feel like they should be given grades and incentives, when in fact, they have not worked enough to receive any of it. Being okay with the bare minimum to pass is not acceptable, but our students believe that it is. Some of our students do not even see the importance of getting a good, free education. This is not acceptable by any means. We must rally behind our students and let them know that education is indeed important and no matter what, it is needed to be successful in life.

Now granted, not all students have the same ability level academically and that is ok, we are all different. With knowing your child's academic ability level, comes knowing what areas they are good in and knowing what areas they struggle in, so that you are able to accommodate their needs in order for them to be successful. If I know that my child is not a great math student, I am going to be on him to make sure he feels comfortable with what is going on in the class. If he is struggling, then I will know that I need to get him some assistance. Often times, students are "scared" for whatever reason to speak up and say they do not understand a certain concept or ask for any help in the classroom. It seems as if they would rather struggle and get behind, than stay for after school tutoring with the teacher, because it may not be seen as being cool by their peers. We cannot allow this to happen. We have to keep communication open with our children, and the teachers, to stay on top of what is going on. Now, on the flip side, if my child is outstanding in an area, I know that I do not have to worry so much about the grade in that class. As parents, when it comes to academics, we have to stay on top of checking grades just as much as the student needs to stay on top of making the grades, and being successful.

If you have a child that receives special education services, there is no difference. Knowing what your child struggles in, and knowing what their academic ability levels are, is vital to their success. Attending IEP (Individualized Educational Plan) meetings, knowing what services your child is to receive for the classroom and for testing makes all the difference in their success. Because a student with an IEP is already struggling academically or behaviorally, they must have that extra help to stay on track. When a child brings home a bad grade, don't be so quick to assume they didn't study or they were just being lazy. It could very well be that they just don't understand the work. If you know your child's ability level, you will be able to determine which it really is, and offer the assistance that will help them, and not make them shutdown. All students are capable of learning, but all learn at different paces. Support your student, know their ability level, and help them be successful. Always keep in mind, core academics count. Now, let's talk athletically.

Think back to when your child was starting to play sports and they would be out on the field, court, etc.; you would push them to keep going and cheer them on, and help keep them focused when the game didn't go so well for them. When your child's team would win, there would be a great celebration. When your child's team would lose, there would always be a talk about it being okay to lose, and you just need to work harder the next time. Yes, I have had several of those talks and still have those talks as often as needed. As time goes on, and your child begins to take a more vested interest in a certain sport, you take the necessary steps to make sure they have what they need to pursue this sport. You invest your time, money, research the best program, and even get personal coaches to give your child the upper hand with their sport. Some parents spend time year round going from one sport to the other because their child is just that into it, and they are supportive of their ambitions. I definitely support parents that do this, as I did for several years until my son took a special interest in basketball, and that was the only sport we focused on, still year round, but just that sport alone. In knowing your child's athletic ability you must know when they really want to pursue something and when they are just doing it for fun. Now, this may take some time to come to know and that is okay. As your child goes through school, being involved in different sports can be good because it keeps them structured, and gives them something to work harder for. Student-athletes have to maintain passing grades to be able to play in a sport. This is regulated by high school rules, governed by the state athletic association, as well as by the coach of that particular sport.

Playing a sport as a freshman can be very challenging if there is no discipline in the student to maintain academics, and to be on top of their game in their chosen sport. Once this is realized and a schedule is set on how to be a great student and athlete, it should get easier for the student. Freshman and sophomore years are spent bringing it together and learning the pattern needed to be successful in both areas. Once a child gets to their junior and senior years in high school, it is time to sit down and determine if this sport is something they want to pursue beyond high school. It is okay if they do not, this is something I had to come to terms with myself. I have always supported my child with his basketball, paying plenty of money for him to do so, but as time went on, I began to ask myself if this is something he really wanted to pursue after high school. I always had great relationships with the coaches and would reach out to them for their opinion and listen to them about my son's ability level as they saw it. Now, as a parent, because our kids are our world, we may not always agree with the coaches, however, they are the ones who work day in and day out with our kids and know their ability level in that sport, because it's what they do.

We may think that our child can do something great, when in actuality it may not be as great as we think when compared to other students. As great as we think our child may be able to handle a ball and play like LeBron James or Stephen Curry, they may not be able to handle the ball like we think they can. When you sit down and speak with a coach who has years and years of experience evaluating kids and knowing what it takes to make it to that next level, you find out the truth. We have to learn to play our role as parents and let the coaches, who know the game, do what they know how to do. I will address this later. There is a lot to be said on that alone.

Getting back to knowing your child's ability level, in their junior and senior years, you will be able to tell if your child wants to take their love of playing the game (whatever the game may be) even further. A child that wants to pursue a sport in college will be dedicated to doing what it takes to grow in that area. This means, early rise to practice, extra work out sessions, doing small things in between to develop skills in any area needed. This dedication has to be something they do on their own. Although you can encourage them along, you cannot make them do this, it has to come from within. It cannot be you getting them up every morning saying, "It's time to go work out," or "You need to get ready for practice," this is not what dedication looks like. They have to want it for themselves, and see the need to work hard for it without being told to do so.

You will be able to tell if your child has that passion, or if they are just enjoying playing the sport for leisure. Understand there is a difference between being supportive for something they want to do and having to push them to do something that you think they should do. You have to keep an open mind about your child's future. I can honestly say that becoming more realistic about your child's ability to play at the next level will make the process of post-graduation decisions a little easier for you, as parents and for your student. I say this because even if your child decides to go to college and not pursue a sport, knowing what direction to take is a great feeling, and time is not wasted. By this I mean, if you are pushing your child to play a sport that they may not want to pursue on the next level, you waste valuable time and resources trying to find the "right" spot for them because that is what you think they should do. I believe there is a fit for everyone as far as post-secondary options go speaking as an educator. I can say that playing a collegiate level sport may not be the route for your child, and that is perfectly fine. There is nothing wrong with playing a sport for years, as a child, during middle and high school, and then realizing that it is not what you want to pursue. Focusing on academics alone is not a bad thing for a student-athlete. At least, they know what they want to do and can start their journey as a college student focused on doing just that. Remember, understanding your child's ability level will help you in the end in many different ways.

Always be honest with yourself and with your child, take the advice of the coaches who coach your child and know the game. More than anything, stay on top of academics and be an all-around supporter of your child's own dreams, not allowing your dreams from them to overshadow theirs.

Levels of Collegiate Competition

Once your child has decided that they indeed would like to pursue their chosen sport beyond high school, and you have come to grips with their ability level, it is time to decide which collegiate level they will participate in based on talent and academics. There are approximately 350 Division I schools, over 300 Division II, over 400 Division III, over 250 NAIA, over 500 NJCAA. I know these acronyms may not mean anything now, but I will give you information about each level to give you a clear understanding of each level's requirements. I will also say that just because you or your child thinks they are Division 1 material, doesn't mean they are. Division I is the best of the best talent and a student-athlete has to prove they are worth it. There is, however, a fit for each athlete that wishes to pursue their sport at the next level.

There are three NCAA Divisions. **Division I** (DI) level schools are larger, with more facilities and degree programs to offer a student-athlete because of the large athletic budgets, and more scholarship money available. In Division I, academics are set at a higher standard for athletes to show readiness for college curriculum. Most athletes feel they are Division I material, but are not prepared for the rigors of a college athlete.

21

Athletes have to prove they have the talent, dedication, and drive to succeed, and are worth the time and the money colleges have to offer. Someone of significance should make some type of evaluation as to the talent that is shown in your athlete's specific sport. By someone of significance, I am referring to a coach, recruiter, a ranking service, or former player. But no need to worry about that right now, we will discuss that later. Getting recognized for your abilities doesn't start during your senior year of high school, it is something that you have to work at from the moment you begin to play sports, and even more when it is decided to concentrate on a certain sport.

Colleges look at the overall athletic abilities of their recruits and what that athlete brings to the table. Good academics, along with leadership abilities, and a great attitude are required qualities. If the work ethic is there, it is a great opportunity to become a part of a D1 program. Examples of DI schools are the University of Kentucky (one of my favorites), University of Alabama, University of Arizona, Florida State University, University of Georgia, Savannah State University, Purdue University, Grambling State University, Central Michigan University, and Duke University. These schools qualify for Division I status by sponsoring at least 7 sports for both men and women. The qualifying standards to participate is higher than the other divisions. Division 1 schools are great schools to attend to further your education, along with athletic aspirations. They are big business, with lots of incentives, and are constantly looking for student-athletes to help them generate money and exposure. If your student-athlete does not have what it takes for a Division I school, there are still other options that will fit his/her talents. Let's look at the next level.

Division II schools offer scholarships as well, but may not cover as much as Division I schools. When it comes to getting a scholarship from a DII school, it will be a scholarship that is a mixture of athletic aid, academic aid, and grants that may be available. Enrollment sizes at a DII schools are less which makes for a better academic arrangement for someone that just does not want the larger campus life style, and still be able to get a competitive experience in their chosen sport. DII schools are for those athletes who may need more development or academic assistance, but still have a very strong commitment to continue their athletic endeavors, and enjoy being competitive. The focus is on the student-athlete as a whole. Being able to manage their time for academics as well as their time for practices and meetings is very critical.

Division II schools provide athletes with less academic pressures than Division I. Some DII schools are Tuskegee University, University of West Florida, Albany State University in Georgia, Clark Atlanta University, Morehouse College, Kentucky State University, Livingston College, Walsh University, Benedict College, and Virginia State University. The important thing to keep in mind is that attending any school is great because it shows that your student-athlete is committed to furthering their academic career and possibly their athletic career. It's good to always have options when it comes to taking control of life. At the end of the day, it is about the big picture, no matter the route chosen, having the big picture goal in mind determines success. Always encourage your student-athlete to do the best they can; it brings character and work ethic that help lead to their ultimate goal.

The last classification under the NCAA umbrella is **Division III**. The important thing to know about DIII schools is that they do not offer athletic scholarships. However, there are other forms of aid available for your student-athlete. Remember I stated in the start of this chapter, there are over 400 DIII schools. This classification makes up the largest

NCAA division as it relates to schools and the number of participants. Academics are the primary focus when it comes to attending a Division III institution. It is a balance of academic challenges and athletic goals to further your ambitions. You are a student first regardless of anything else. You are not going to be the big man/woman on campus as it pertains to sports because the focus is academics first. The practice and playing seasons for DIII schools are shorter than all other divisions due to the importance and attention giving to academics. This gives student-athletes more time to focus on their studies. When attending a DIII school, student-athletes are not bound by the obligations that receiving an athletic scholarship holds. They are students, period, who are taught the life skills that will make them more valuable as citizens and entrepreneurs. It teaches them discipline, teamwork, leadership, and how to persevere during hard times when things don't go as planned.

A few of the Division III schools include Oglethorpe University, Berry College, University of Chicago, Saint Mary's College (Indiana), Wabash College, Louisiana College, John Hopkins University, Salem College, Buffalo State, State University of New York, Medgar Evers College, University of Mount Union, Johnson & Wales University (RI), University of Dallas.

Remember, academic success is at the forefront of DIII schools; classroom ethics and values stand out. While many student-athletes will always say they are DI material, we know as parents, that it takes a lot of time, talent, and dedication to make it to that level. Attending a DII or DIII school is not a bad thing, it just depends on the student-athletes knowing what's best for them according to the level of talent they possess. If one of the NCAA Division schools does not work, there are still other options available to fit the needs of the lower profile student-athlete.

The next level of competition that is available to participate in would be **NAIA** (National Association of Intercollegiate Athletics), which is comprised of more than 250 schools. Athletic aid is available at NAIA schools and you have to be eligible to receive this assistance. Like the NCAA, there is an eligibility center for the NAIA as well. I will discuss the NCAA eligibility requirements later. The NAIA eligibility requires a certain ACT (18) and SAT (860) score to be considered, as well as a certain grade point average (2.0). Taking either of these tests are key to college acceptance, whether an athlete or not. The SAT and ACT will be discussed in depth later as well. NAIA schools are competitive in their own rights.

Although most of the schools are smaller in size, they give your student-athlete an opportunity to continue their athletic dreams. Student-athletes are the center of the NAIA organization and guide many of its decisions. With the NAIA rules, your student-athlete will compete against other student-athletes that have similar levels of training, meaning the playing field is always leveled for your student-athlete.

To give you an idea of some NAIA schools, here are a few. College of Coastal Georgia, Fisk University, Life University, Marian University, Ohio Christian University, Pacific Union College, and Saint Xavier University are all a part of the NAIA family. This list only gives you an idea of the type of schools that are included in the NAIA division, there are many more to choose from. As stated before, although your child may think they are NCAA Division I quality, it is up to you to give them options that truly fit their talent level, keeping in mind that the overall idea is for them to be able to continue their education and sport after high school, getting your student-athlete to realize their best chance at success may not always be at a DI, DII, or even DIII school. Starting at a lower division school does not mean they can't later transfer into another school if they become ready and qualify academically to participate at a higher level of competition. The rules on transfers can be very tricky and contacting the said schools is always best when making an informed decision.

The **NJCAA** (National Junior College Athletic Association) is a program that is designed to give your student-athlete a place to start. This may be for the students who academically are not ready for a four year institution and want to take on a much smaller setting to get a smoother start. NJCAA schools, which are broken into Divisions, can offer athletic scholarships to its student-athletes, whether being full or partial awards. The eligibility requirements for NJCAA are simple; graduate from high school, have a general education diploma or a state department of education approved high school equivalency test, be an amateur that has not exhausted eligibility with any other institution, and be in good health. With scholarships, Division 1 NJCAA schools may grant full athletic scholarships, Division II may grant scholarships limited to tuition, books, and fees, and Division III do not offer any athletic scholarships.

There over 500 NJCAA colleges to choose from. Each school has its own set of eligibility requirements (academically and athletically), so contacting the admissions and/or athletic department of the school of interest would be highly recommended to get all of the information straight from the source. NJCAA is another alternative student-athletes could choose until they are academically and athletically able to enter into another institution of a higher level. No matter what decision is made, there is something for everyone to be able to further their education and continue their athletic goals at the development stage they need.

This chapter has been all about giving you some insight into the various post-graduation options that are available for your student-athlete to be able to continue playing the game they have grown to love and want to pursue. The information given here is just a sampling of all the information that is available for you to gain more knowledge, but this gives you the basic ideas to guide you to further research, ask certain questions, speak with your student-athlete and devise a plan. Always keep in mind that it is about having options, being ready when opportunities present themselves, and having a plan B when plan A just doesn't work out. It is never the end for an athlete who thinks all is lost because they did not get into that number one school they have been dreaming of all of their high school career. The big picture needs to be a constant thought, and although their big picture may be similar to someone else's, there are various ways of getting the same results in the end. As a parent, we have to understand what fits our student-athletes and help guide them. Often time, they have their sights set on things they just aren't ready for, but with hard work, they can accomplish their goals of being a better student-athlete all around. It starts very early with academics and being dedicated to keeping grades up and being a star athlete on and off the field. I hope that you have found this information to be helpful to you. There is so much more to discuss. As we move forward, we will tackle the things that can help you and your student-athlete get into that top school of choice. Of course, when it comes to athletics, talent definitely is the deciding factor for receiving athletic scholarships but not for academics, which will always takes precedence. Let's continue on, taking a look at the SAT or ACT test. These test are very important as they are needed to obtain entrance into colleges and to be eligible under the NCAA.

SAT/ACT Testing

Okay parents, this chapter is going to be very vital to the success of your child getting into college and obtaining scholarships, whether academically or athletically. In this chapter, we will discuss the two types of test that colleges use as a requirement for admission, how they are structured, and which one may be best for your child to take. I will also touch briefly on the NCAA requirements when taking these test, but not too much because I will go more in depth to all NCAA requirements in later. The focus of this section is to get you familiar with each test and how they are used, so let's get started. Parents, depending on where you went to high school you may be more familiar with one test than the other. For me, I grew up in Kentucky and I took the ACT. I was not as familiar with the SAT. Most colleges accept either one when it comes to gaining admission. Now, the score that each school requires will differ. We will look at the ACT test first.

Historically known as the American College Test, now just simply ACT is a college readiness assessment that helps a student see just where they stand when it comes to being ready for college. The ACT is used by colleges in a number of ways. One of the most important ways is for college admissions, which helps admission offices determine which students can benefit the most from the various programs they offer. Other ways the ACT is used by colleges include placement in various courses using scores, academic advisement, and even some scholarships and other forms of aid use the score as part of their determination to assist a student. The ACT is comprised of four multiple-choice test in the subject areas of English, Mathematics, Reading, and Science. There is also a writing portion of the ACT, but it is not always required by colleges, so check with your student-athlete's college of choice when deciding to take the writing portion of the test. Each section of the test is broken down into different time constraints. A student needs to really time themselves out to be able to answer each question in the different section so they will have the ample amount of time to complete each section.

The English section has 75 questions and students are given 45 minutes to complete this section. The English section will measure Standard English usage and mechanics along with rhetorical skills. The Mathematics section has 60 questions and students are given 60 minutes to complete this section. The Math section evaluates skills in Pre-Algebra, Elementary to Intermediate Algebra, Coordinate Geometry, Plane Geometry and

Trigonometry based problems. High school Geometry is normally not taken until 10th grade year, which is why I always suggest to parents to start your child taking the ACT the second semester of their 10th grade year. With taking it at this time, you can get a feel for where you stand and know what to study for the next time. There are no limits to the number of times you take the ACT, the best score will be used. The Reading section of the test consists of 40 questions and students are given 35 minutes to complete this section. The Reading section measures reading comprehension on skills in Social Studies, Natural Sciences, Arts and Literature. The last section of the ACT is the Science portion, which contains 40 questions with 35 minutes to complete those questions as well. In this section of the test, students are assessed on skills in interpretation, analysis, evaluation, reasoning, and problem-solving skills. Keep in mind that the ACT has a writing portion with it as well that is optional. The writing portion of the test measures writing skills learned in high school and what students may see in an entry-level college course.

Now, let's take a look at how the ACT is scored. I have given you the number of questions in each section, so the first thing in scoring is to take the number of correct answers from each section and count them up first.

One great thing about the ACT is that they do not deduct for wrong answers, so students are not penalized for guessing an answer. Always tells your students to make sure they answers all the questions on the ACT, they may just get it right even when they had to guess and this will only help them, not hurt them. After counting up the correct answers, the raw scores are converted to scale scores. ACT scores are converted from raw to scale scores in order for a comparison to be made between various test versions and all its test takers. Scale scores have the same meaning no matter what form of test, date of test, or set of questions on test.

Moving on, keep in mind a raw score is the total number of correct answers in a section. A scale score is what you receive on each section of a test when looked at on a chart that is used by ACT. Each official ACT test has its own chart, on a scale of 1 to 36. After this is done, students receive what is called the composite score, which is the average of the four scaled scores, with 36 being the highest possible score. There is also a sum score given and this is the score that matters with the NCAA. An ACT sum score is calculated by adding English, Math, Reading and Science sub scores. The minimum needed to be eligible for athletic aid per NCAA is 75 provided you have the needed grade point average. There are charts available to give you an estimate of what your score may be, but it will not be exact, as the ACT uses their own variation for each test. Ever wonder why scores need to be converted in the first place? The conversion is done to ensure that the level of difficulty across each test shows a slight variation. This means that an ACT test taken in February will show the same level of skills as a test taken in April. I hope this has made it a little clearer as to the ACT test, why students need to take it, how it is scored and how the scores are used. Students can take an ACT test as many times as needed to gain the score required to obtain admissions to the school of their choosing. The composite scores is what matters the most. Last thing about ACT, it is offered 6 times a year, and takes about 3 hours and 40 mins to complete including the essay. It can cost $34.00-$49.50, and can be covered with a fee waiver if you qualify. More information to come later in this section on fee waivers. Alright, I think that will get you all set with ACT, let's move right along to the SAT test.

Just like the ACT, the SAT was originally known as the Scholastic Assessment Test, now it is just simply the SAT. The SAT, which was redesigned and newly released in March 2016, is used for college admission as well. The newly designed SAT mirrors the ACT in that students are no longer penalized for incorrect answers and the essay is optional, I personally love this change. The SAT now has more reasoning problems for the students to work through, using linear and sequential fashion. What this means, is that a student's ability to process information quickly and solve a problem will be very vital to being successful with the newly designed SAT. Another major change is the SAT now only offers 4 answer choices versus the 5 choices on the test prior to March 2016. Of course when things change, there will be certain aspects that people will not like about it. The newly designed SAT (March 2016) requires students to follow multiple steps to get an answer. There is more complex structure and vocabulary on the Reading portion, foundational Math skills will need to be stronger as well as reasoning and critical thinking skills will need to be top notch. While there are fewer sections on the SAT than before, the sections are longer in time. Let's go ahead and take a closer look.

The SAT has 2 sections, Evidence-Based Reading and Writing section and a Math section. The length of the test is 3 hours without essay and about 3 hours and 50 minutes with essay, this is without breaks. The SAT can be taken as a pencil and paper test or as a computer test. For the Evidence-

Based Reading and Writing section, there are two separate test, Reading is one focus and Writing and Language is the other. These sections focus on multiple-meaning words. The passages draw from significant historical or scientific documents, which may include charts or graphs, so paying attention in History and Science will be very important for your student. The Reading passages are structured with complexity and the vocabulary is strong. The grammar used is based on the passages, and punctuation is emphasized as well. The Math section focuses on higher-level math that includes Trigonometry and it is more application-based, with multiple step questions as stated before. The core Math competencies are heavily emphasized, meaning turning Math into English and English into Math. To do well on this section, a student will need to have a deep understanding of the theories behind actual Mathematical principles. There are also grid-in questions that require extended-thinking and are worth more points, which brings us to the timing and scoring of the SAT. The reading section has 52 questions and students are allotted 65 minutes to complete. The writing and language section has 44 questions and students are allotted 35 minutes to complete. The Math section has 58 questions with 80 minutes to complete, making the full SAT have 154 questions and 180 minutes in length without the essay. The essay portion of the test, if taken, has a 50 minute allotment and students are asked to analyze a passage and how the author built their argument.

Scoring of the SAT uses raw scores because there is no penalty for guessing. The raw scores are then converted to scale scores on a scale of 200 to 800 using a process called equating. With equating, adjustments are made for slight differences in difficulty between various versions of the test. This is done to make sure there is no advantage in taking the test on a different day. So even though the questions may be different on a different test date, a score of 40 means the same no matter what, just as with the ACT. The highest score for the SAT is 1600, obtaining 800 on both sections. With the level of math that the SAT includes, students may not be introduced to it until their junior year, but your student may take it before then if they are prepared, or just want to see how well they do. The SAT score report will breakdown your results with more detail and will provide an explanation for you. The main thing to consider is the total score for each section.

The last focus with scoring is sending scores to interested colleges. When taking the SAT, you receive four score reports which allows you to send your scores to four institutions of your choice without a fee. When you register for the SAT, it will ask for the names of the colleges your student wants to receive your scores, look up the school codes and submit. There is a nine day window to submit schools to receive free report. On the 10th day, there is a fee requires unless your student is eligible for a SAT waiver, they can send up to four more reports for free. If your student-athlete has any intentions on playing a sport after high school one of the most important codes will be "9999", as this is the code for the NCAA to receive test scores, this code is the same for SAT and ACT.

I mentioned fee waivers, a student in the 11th or 12th grade may be eligible for a fee waiver to take the SAT or ACT if they meet certain criteria. If a student meets any of the following criteria; (1) enrolled in or eligible to participate in the National School Lunch Program (NSLP), (2) annual family income falls within the Income Eligibility Guidelines set by USDA Food and Nutrition Service, (3) enrolled in a federal, state, or local program that aids students from low-income families, (4) family receives public assistance, (5) lives in federal subsidized public housing or a foster home, or are homeless, and (6) a ward of the state or an orphan. The fee waivers cover the fee for up to two SAT test, with or without essay. It can also cover up to two SAT subject tests, which are mainly used to help in course placement in certain subject areas. Please reach out to particular colleges to know if SAT subject test are recommended.

With the ACT, students are also eligible for up to two waivers and can send up to four score reports to colleges as well. The college application waivers are used in lieu of paying college application fees. Not all colleges accept application waivers, research will need to be done to confirm if the schools of interest accepts waivers. The National Association for College Admission Counseling (NACAC) is also a great tool to use for research and direction in choosing a post- secondary institution. Also, fee application waivers are available through them if certain qualifications are met.

Alright, I hope this section has given you better insight into the two different test that are available for students to take to gain college admissions. Like anything, once students have taken both test, they can get a feel for which test they may perform better on. Once the determination is made, they can choose to focus on taking that test only.

Being prepared for these test will make all the difference. Getting extra tutoring or taking a prep class is never a bad idea. There are many free websites that can be used to study for either test before you decide to pay big bucks for a name. Attending tutoring from the math and language teachers at school also is a great way to help prepare for test. Many school systems are now offering ACT and SAT prep classes along with their regular course selections.

Always do your research before spending money, make sure your student is actually studying and knows what is on the test and how to take the test (i.e.-answering all questions without penalty, and using time wisely), these small things count. Please see the back of book for a listing of helpful websites regarding the ACT and SAT. Good luck to your student and be supportive of them every step, as testing can be difficult. Remind them to always stay positive and reach for the score required to gain admission to the college of their choice. It is now time to discuss something that no parent likes to hear, allowing the coaches to do their job and coach without parental input on actual coaching style. Keep reading to hear from coaches and what they tell their parents the most and why you should listen.

Let the Coaches Coach

Parents, think back to when you were playing a sport. You would look out into the stands and see your parents. No matter what was going on, you would look to your parents for guidance regardless of what was being said by the coach. If you have played a sport, you have experienced this. This can only get us so far, after growing in the sport, athletes must begin to listen to their coaches instead of their parents. Even if their parents may have been athletes in that sport, they are not with them in daily practice. They do not know the chemistry of the team, and unless they are the actual coach, the parents really have no say in how the team is ran. I know, that as a parent, you give your child advice and can tell them how things were for you, but the truth of the matter is, you can only "coach" your student-athlete as an individual. When he gets with his team, it is the coach that he needs to listen to. Not all coaches will do what you as the parent feel they should do, and that is fine. How a coach runs his/her team is up to them and their staff.

I have several friends who coach that I communicate with and the biggest thing I hear from them is concerning the parents. No matter what the sport is, coaches always say the parents can be worse than the athletes at times. My dear friend Darius Hodge, Head Basketball Coach from Hiram High School in Hiram, Georgia, stated, "Parents need to allow their student-athletes to be coached." What this means is that as parents, we have to allow them to be coached hard, not make up excuses for them even when they are making mistakes. I know this can be hard to do because you think you know what is best for your children at all times, but the truth of the matter is that once your children get to middle and high school, you have to let go of what you think should be done on the court or field, and allow the coaches to do their jobs.

How would you like it if someone was at your job on a daily basis telling you exactly what to do and how to do it? I am quite sure, you would not like this at all, none of us would, so why do this with coaches. The coaches are in place for a reason and you have to allow them to do what you trust they will do with your student-athletes. It takes a lot of time and dedication to be a coach of any sport. Coaches want to see their student-athletes succeed just as much as the parents do. When building or trying to maintain a solid athletic program, coaches have a lot to deal with. Having supportive parents that do not question every single move can help to alleviate some of that stress that comes along with coaching.

There will be times when you feel like the coach isn't giving your student-athlete the time and attention you feel he deserves, but that's just it, you feel that way. When the coaches make a decision, they have good reason to and if the rules of the program have been stated to parents and players, there is no discussion needed.

So what is the coach's real job you ask? The job of a coach could be many things to many different people, but the basis is always the same; to help improve the skills and abilities of athletes in the particular sport. A coach cannot get your child to the NBA, NFL, or any other major league sport. Your student-athlete has to want it for themselves and be coachable. The coach is there to lead them in the right direction and teach them the fundamentals needed to get there, but they have to be willing to listen and follow through. When your student is in high school, coaches should also be helping to keep the student-athlete on track academically by checking grades and giving consequences when grades are not up to par. There are normally high school rules and regulations put in place that student-athletes have to follow to become and remain eligible to play a sport. It is up to the student-athletes to maintain grades in order to remain on the active roster for any high school sport. Along with checking academics, coaches of course want to develop student-athletes to reach their best potential. With developing student-athletes comes time and energy that the coaches must give to each athlete to become the best they can and prepare for a possible future in that sport after high school. Many high school coaches spend countless hours in and out of the game to help their student-athletes. A good coach will have talks with his athletes about life in general and not just sports. They will encourage their athletes to be the best they can be in all areas of life. A great coach has a well-rounded team, but again, your student-athlete has to be coachable and have respect for the coach and the game itself.

Once your student-athlete gets to be a junior or senior, the coach should be focusing on getting them to the next level if this is their desire and their talent supports it. Many student-athletes, as I have stated, feel they may be Division I material when in reality they just are not. A coach knows the talent level of his players, and what level would best fit them when it comes to moving forward after high school. While not all coaches will work as hard as others for their student-athletes, they are definitely a starting point to assist your student with getting to the next level. Now, keep in mind, it is not solely up to the coach to get your child recruited. As the parent, you have to be able to get your child exposure by going to camps and various events that will put your athletes in front of people that are able to assist them with getting to the next level, we will discuss this later.

I reached out to a few other coaches on what they see most with parents when it comes to coaching and how they handle it when it comes to their players. In speaking with Patrice Bryant, Head Girls Basketball Coach at Langston Hughes High School in Fairburn, Georgia, she stated, "Players get their playing time from practice. If they can't prove to me that they can do the right thing in practice, then I definitely can't trust them to do the right thing during the game. Practices are open to all parents. If they want to see why their child is not playing they can come to practice." She makes a valid point here because a coach has to be able to depend on student-athletes to produce, and if they are not showing up in practice then playing time will definitely be limited. When this happens, there is nothing a parent can say to a coach about it. The conversation needs to be held with the athlete.

Parents have to keep in mind that coaching takes a lot because every athlete is different. Whether you believe it or not, the background of an athlete plays a very important part in it all. What an athlete has to deal with outside of the sport has an affect on them with the sport and this can make it harder for a coach to reach that child's potential. What if a child does not have the resources to practice outside of school or to get to other functions that will allow him to get more practice? The only practice he may get is with the coach. These are all things that a coach has to take into consideration, and if your student-athlete has a coach that understands these things, they will do all in their power to see that the child's outside factors are not a hindrance to his athletic skills and developments. Having a supportive parent helps this and allows the coach more ground to do what is needed to successfully help each athlete. The coaching your child receives in high school is minor compared to the coaching they will receive at the next level.

College coaches have to be able to depend on student-athletes to play the game and not be affected by small things; they have to be able to listen and follow through without giving attitude or unnecessary feedback. Corry Black, from Columbus, Georgia, created and runs CB Hoops, an organization designed to help student-athletes in their quest to play College Basketball. Corry is a former College Basketball Coach and knows what it takes for student-athletes to get recruited and earn a chance to play at the next level. In speaking with Corry, he stated the one thing he tells all athletes he works with is this, "If you don't put in the work, it won't work!" Student-athletes have to know that it takes hard work and dedication to make it because you are not only going up against other athletes in your region, but athletes from all over the country possibly. It is not different from sport to sport, they all require that top notch dedication to stand out above the rest. In talking with Terrone Owens, Offensive Coordinator at Lamar County High School in Barnesville, Georgia, about how parents can be, he stated, "Parents have to allow us to do our jobs and if they don't, they can do it, but it will not bring results needed to help their student-athlete in the end."

At the beginning of each season, no matter the sport, a parent meeting is held. At this parent meeting, the guidelines are set for what the coach expects of his players and what he expects from his parents. When everyone walks away from this meeting, it should be clear as to how things will go, but this is not always the case. There are always the parents who just will not take what has been stated plainly and let it be; they have to challenge everything and approach the coach with unnecessary issues. Each coach has their own coaching philosophy and it is the golden rule, bringing an issue to the head coach will not make this change. In fact, it may hinder it more. There are chains of command that should be in place with each athletic program and you will get further following those than not. Once in high school, players should be able to effectively communicate with their coaches on their own. A relationship has to be built with the coach and player to create a level of independency for the athlete and trust between the both of them. During my student-athlete's high school years, there were plenty of times I wondered why. Why was he not in the game, why did he not go to this side of the court, why didn't he go in for a layup instead of attempting a 3 point shot, why didn't he pass the ball; all these questions were in my head at one point in time. However, the one thing, I knew not to do was to question the coach.

My first questions would always be to my student-athlete as to what was going on. Being in the stands, you never know what has been said between the player and the coach before the game or at any point as to what needs to be done during the game to help the team as a whole. Parents have to be supportive of the coach and the child in a manner in which everyone wins. Be respectful of the coach's position and know that they are in place to help your student-athlete progress and move to the next level should that be their goal. Nobody is perfect and each play of every game will not be executed the way you want it to, there will be off days for everyone involved. The main thing to remember is that the learning experience will always be there with a win and with a loss. It is about getting back out there and making the next time a better one. Student-athletes have to learn to take the good with the bad, learn to listen to the coach, and make each moment count.

When asked about being a parent to a Division I student- athlete when it came to the coaches' decisions, Anthony Hickey, Head Girls Basketball Coach at Christian County High School in Hopkinsville, Kentucky, whose son played basketball at Louisiana State University and Oklahoma State University stated, "I didn't live through my son, I allowed my son to learn and grow to make his own decisions in life. I was there to support and encourage him every step of the way." Hickey' son, Anthony Hickey Jr. currently plays professional basketball overseas in Poland with the Asseco Gdynia. So as you can see, you don't have to be the frontrunner in all that your kids experience. You can be supportive of them and allow them to make mistakes, learn from them and be right there to support them. It is very imperative to allow the coaches to coach and you be the parent that supports the program as a whole and not feel certain ways when things are not going in your favor as it relates to your student-athlete. Student-athletes have enough to deal with in trying to maintain academics and play a sport, without the hassle of knowing Mom or Dad will always make a scene with the coach about what did or didn't happen during a game. Please don't do this to your athlete. Support your student-athletes and allow the coaches to coach.

Exposure and Recruiting

Parents, recruiting and exposure is an important part of what it will take to get your student-athlete to the next level, based on their skill level. Notice, I said where their skill level takes them, not where they think they should be. When it comes to recruiting, there are several companies that can assist in helping to get your child recruited. These companies can cost a lot of money, but they are capable of getting student-athletes exposure on a wider scale. The first thing is to make sure that you have film. This film can come from actual high school games, which is best, or from other organized sports functions such as AAU games, training sessions, camp sessions, and other events that show the talent of your athlete. Some coaches like to see full games to get an all-around idea of how an athlete plays through a full game, not just their best highlights of them. The full picture of their playing skills need to be seen in order for coaches to make an informed decision about the talent of the student-athlete and what they can offer them. Most coaches who are truly interested in an athlete will make a visit to the school or game to see them in person, or send a staff member to do so, when the rules say they can do so.

When looking at the various ways to get exposure for your student-athlete, many people think about AAU events. AAU (Amateur Athletic Union) is a non-profit amateur sports organization that is dedicated to promoting and developing amateur sports and Physical fitness programs. AAU programs are found in various sports and across the country. AAU can give athletes great exposure if participation in the right events is taken seriously. The school season is only so long and if any student-athlete wants to continuously work on their skill, they have to take part in some other type of events to do so.

If AAU is the organization of choice, it's best to have an upfront conversation with the coach about what you are trying to achieve out of playing. It is always good to do your own research on the events that the coach signs the team up for, if it's not a team sponsored event. AAU sports are used to compete with other talent around the country to draw conclusions. I support AAU sanctioned sports if done properly and by this I mean the players being the center of attention. Some coaches can be in it for the wrong reasons, but the main reason should be for the betterment of the student-athletes, not the coach and staff. In doing your own research about events, see how long the events have been going on, who comes to the events, what reviews may be about the sponsors of the events. Keep in mind that not all exposure is good exposure and if you are spending money, you want to make it worth it. Now, if putting your student-athlete in an additional situation is a problem, other options for extra exposure can be used to get a coaches attention.

AAU can be very costly and requires a lot of travel. If this is not something you are willing or able to do, then getting your student-athlete with a trainer in their sport would be another option to look into. There are numerous organizations that provide training as well as individuals that provide training. The cost for these training sessions will vary depending on what is included. With training, you want to make sure your athlete is developing his skills, not just learning the basics and nothing more. You always want to see some development and if this is not seen, I would find another trainer. A trainer has to communicate with you and your athlete about what the focus of the sessions will be and show consistency. When dealing with a personal trainer in any sport, you will know when it is a good fit for you and your student-athlete, or when they are not. Word of mouth is one of the best ways to find a good trainer because you can hear the results straight from someone who has trained with that person in said sport. Recording these training sessions is always a great idea, as this gives you and your student-athlete the time to reflect on what was learned and to see if growth is occurring, and what needs to take place next to help support the next phase of learning. It is not difficult to find a trainer for your student-athlete, but like anything else, the proper research needs to be done before you invest your time and money into anyone. So, if personal training is not necessarily your thing either, and you would rather just have your athlete get the seasonal training from his sport and spend the rest of the time attending camps to get that extra exposure, that it perfectly okay. Let's take a look at camps and how they can be beneficial.

Camps are held all over the United States and much like AAU, they require some travel for the better ones. Camps are normally a great way to get exposure in front of college coaches who can make some decisions about the talent your student possess. Camps or showcases have college coaches that come out to evaluate the talent and if interested they will make contact with the player. At most camp/showcase, the coaches are provided a list of all participants and a way to identify them as they play games are during the session. The showcases vary in price and some of the smaller showcases may be more valuable for your student-athlete to attend than some of the major ones; it truly depends on the level of play your student-athlete is trying to reach. Most high school coaches are aware of some of the more reputable camps to attend that actually do what they say they will do for your child. For the camps that do not have live coaches attending, they will send out film to coaches, or the coaches have access to their database where they upload film from the sessions. When you sign up for a showcase and you think you're going to see a lot of college coaches and you end up seeing none, this is not always a bad thing. Depending on the time and the season, many coaches are choosing to watch film and reach out that way. You have to keep in mind that coaches are recruiting from all over the United States possibly and not just in your area; therefore, they have to maximize time, and watching film allows them to do this. Not to mention, they have periods in which they can do certain things. Will discuss this later.

The more major showcases such as Nike Basketball Showcase in Chicago or the Nike Football SPARQ Combine are ones that cost and require travel but can bring about great results if the talent is there. The MVP Camp is a great one for football and is cost effective. The Opening Regionals is another one sponsored by Nike that is great to attend for football. When attending camps, athletes have to be ready to give their best and understand they are coming in contact with some of the best from across the United States. Often times, student-athletes feel they are good in comparison to other athletes in their region, not realizing that when it comes to camps, they are attended by student-athletes from all over with a wide range of talent. Attending camps/combines are a great way to really see what level of talent your student-athlete may possess when performing with other talented athletes.

Student-athletes can't be recruited without any exposure. It is all about getting out there, and it's about marketing your student-athlete and their talent. Think about it, the only way you are aware of a product or service is by way of commercial, a salesperson, word of mouth, or seeing it for yourself. This is the same concept when it comes to coaches and recruiters seeing your athlete. How will they know about him or her if you don't make them aware? Marketing is key, so that means getting to camps, showcases, and in front of the people that count. In speaking with Coach Tony Dews, Wide Receiver Coach from University of Arizona, he stated, "It is very important for recruits to remain on track academically, for their parents to be involved, and for communication with high school coach to be top notch. All these parts play a major factor in the recruiting process for an athlete." Coach Dews has been doing this for over 16 years and knows exactly how this recruiting game goes.

Once your child enters high school, they can be recruited by coaches and schools. There are rules to the game of recruiting and you as the parent need to be fully aware of them in order to be successful, and not have any negative repercussions when it comes to your student-athlete. The rules mentioned here are for guidance only. Please make sure that you research information for yourself to be completely clear on what is acceptable and what is not. To start, let's take a look at some of the terms you may have heard or will hear when it comes to recruiting your student-athlete. A **contact** is when a college coach says more than hello to a college bound student-athlete, or their parents during a face-to-face contact that does not happen on a college campus. A **contact period** is the time when a college coach may have face-to-face contact with a student-athlete and their parents, visit their high school, watch them compete, write to them or parents, or contact them or the parents by phone.

An **evaluation period** is when a college coach may visit a student-athlete's high school, watch them compete, write to them or parents, or contact them or parents by phone, but may not have any face-to-face contact with student-athletes or parents off the college campus during this time. A **quiet period** is when a college coach can only have face-to face contact with student-athletes or parents on a college campus; coaches may not watch student-athletes compete during this time unless it is on the actual college campus, nor can they visit their high schools. However, during a quiet period, coaches may write to or telephone a student-athlete or parents. A **dead period** is when a coach may not have any face-to-face contact with student-athletes or parents, they may not watch them compete or visit high schools during this time, but they may still write or phone the student-athlete or parents. The above defines what each period is.

Now we will look at when each period occurs for basketball and football seasons. While this information may focus only on these two sports, remember that each sport has their own recruiting calendar. NCAA updates the calendars yearly according to when the specific sport's season occurs. This will give you an idea of those time frames, but actual dates vary year to year. Another important thing to know is exactly what constitutes an official visit. An official visit is happening anytime a college-bound athlete or their parents visit a college campus and the cost of that visit is paid for by the college. During an official (college paid) visit the college can pay for transportation to and from the college for the student-athlete, lodging, plus three meals a day for both the student-athlete and parents, as well as entertainment expense (reasonable) including three tickets to a home sporting event. An unofficial visit would not be paid for by the college. The student-athlete or parents pay all cost of that visit including transportation, lodging, and meals. On an unofficial visit, the college can only give the student-athlete three tickets to a home sporting event. Keep this in mind when you are making plans to visit colleges.

Looking at the recruiting calendars, this will give you some of the key things to know. As I have stated several times, always do your research when it comes down to it. This will guide you and give you some basic knowledge.

For **Division I Football**, as a freshman or sophomore, you can receive questionnaires, camp brochures, nonathletic institutional publications, and any NCAA educational material published by NCAA only. As a junior, you can receive recruiting materials starting September 1, receive electronic communications such as emails and faxes, and you can receive telephone calls during the period of April 15 through May 31, but only one call. As a senior, you can receive one phone call per week starting September 1 or unlimited calls during contact period, which is normally around the end of November through the end of January with the exception of a period from mid-December to mid-January, which is a dead period. As a senior, off-campus contact can occur starting July 1 prior to senior year and is limited to contact periods only. Official visits as a senior may occur opening day of classes. There are evaluation days and contact periods. With football, there are 42 evaluations days during fall evaluation period, and 168 evaluation days during spring evaluation period. There are a limit of three evaluations during an academic year which include, one evaluation during the fall, two evaluations from April 15 through May 31 of which one is used to assess athletic ability and the other to assess academic qualifications. There can be no more than six off-campus contacts per college-bound student-athlete at any place. For football, remember to refer to the calendar that comes out yearly in regards to exact dates for each period (quiet, evaluation, contact, dead) that takes place. The few dates given above are to give you a time frame; **always do your own research**.

Still in the spirit of football, time to take a look at the **Division II Football** recruiting rules. As a freshman or sophomore, a student-athlete can receive questionnaires, camp brochures, nonathletic institutional publications, and any NCAA educational material published by NCAA only. The real recruiting starts junior year. Student-athletes can receive recruiting materials and have off-campus contact as of June 15 of the preceding junior year for a student-athlete. They can also have an official visit and there is no limit to the number of recruiting materials, electronic transmissions, and telephone calls received, provided there is no competition taking place. As of senior year for a Division II prospect, the same rules apply as of junior year, but keep in mind there are dates for each period. Remember to refer to the yearly calendar produced by NCAA for exact dates. For **Division III Football**, rules are less restrictive than the others. As a freshman and sophomore, student-athletes can receive recruiting materials and telephone calls with no limitations. As a junior, they can receive the same plus off-campus contact at the conclusion of their junior year. As a senior, all the above are permitted along with an official visit starting the first day of classes, and there is a limit of one visit per school. There are no restrictions on evaluations or contacts as long as competition is not in play.

With **NAIA Football** recruiting, there are no recruiting rules, no calendars, and no restrictions for high school student-athletes. NAIA schools can make unlimited contact during freshman, sophomore, and junior years to a prospect. As a senior, same rules apply unless the student-athlete has enrolled in another institution.

With the **NJCAA (JUCO) Football,** the rules are pretty simple as well and goes for all sports. There are no recruiting calendars and no gifts can be given other than an athletic scholarship. There are no limits on coaches contacting student-athletes from their freshman to junior years. Senior year, the same rules apply unless the student-athletes has enrolled in another institution. A NJCAA institution may pay for one visit to its campus for the student-athlete for two day and two nights, no longer, and only to the campus and community where campus is located. A NJCAA recruiter may purchase meals for their prospect, but only at the value provided to them by the college. In order to receive an official visit from a NJCAA college, a student-athlete must be a senior and have all credit requirements. If football is your student-athletes' sport of choice, I hope the above information has been helpful to you in some way. Next will be basketball and how it is handled.

For **Division I Basketball**, as a freshman or sophomore, a student-athlete can receive recruiting materials such as questionnaires, camp information, and NCAA materials and nonathletic institutional publications. As of June 15 at the end of sophomore year, all materials are permitted to be received by student-athlete. Telephone calls and electronic communication such as faxes and emails are permitted and can be unlimited beginning June 15 following sophomore year. As a junior, same rules apply with added off-campus contact that can take place as of the opening day of junior classes. Contact may only be made at the student-athletes educational institution with the exception of the recruiting period that normally happens around the beginning of April until mid-April with a few dates that have exceptions.

Just like football, basketball has its own calendars to follow, so make sure you pull these calendars as they change each year accordingly and can be found on the NCAA website. During this recruiting period, a student-athletes can be contacted at their school or at home. Official visit may occur after January 1 of junior year for a prospective student-athlete. As a senior basketball player, all the above rules apply unless a National Letter of Intent has been signed (I will discuss this) or money has been transferred on behalf of the student-athlete in regards to admission.

For basketball, there are more quiet, recruiting, dead, and evaluation periods, so please adhere to calendars for those. The following dates are given as a guide. Beginning of August through first part of September is normally a quiet period, then from September to the first of November is a recruiting period. November also holds a dead period for a few days, then mid-November through March is recruiting time again with a few exceptions in December with a dead period. End of March through first week of April is normally a dead period as well. After that first week of April until the middle, there is a recruiting period with a dead period in it as well as an evaluation period. Near the end of April until the first of July is a quiet period, with the exception of the NBA draft combine. May has a dead period, as does July, so please pull calendars from NCAA when it comes time to go through the process with your student-athlete.

For **Division II Basketball,** as a freshman or sophomore, a student-athlete can receive questionnaires, camp brochures, nonathletic institutional publications, and any NCAA educational material published by NCAA only. Junior year, student-athletes can receive recruiting materials and have off-campus contact as of June 15 of the preceding junior year for a student-athlete. They can also have an official visit and there is no limit to the number recruiting materials received, electronic transmissions, and telephone calls, provided there is no competition taking place. As of senior year for a Division II prospect, the same rules apply as of junior year, but keep in mind there are dates for each period and these dates differ from the above mentioned dates for Division I. Always remember to refer to yearly calendar produced by NCAA for exact dates.

For **Division III Basketball**, as a freshman and sophomore, student-athletes can receive recruiting materials and telephone calls with no limitations. As a junior, they can receive the same plus off-campus contact at the conclusion of their junior year. As a senior, all the above are permitted along with an official visit starting the first day of classes and there is a limit of one visit per school. There are no restrictions on evaluations or contacts as long as competition is not in play.

With **NAIA Basketball** recruiting, there are no recruiting rules, no calendars, and no restrictions for high school student-athletes. NAIA schools can make unlimited contact during freshman, sophomore, and junior years to a prospect. As a senior, same rules apply unless the student-athlete has enrolled in another institution.

With the **NJCAA (JUCO) Basketball,** the rules are pretty simple as well, and again this goes for all sports. There are no recruiting calendars and no gifts can be given other than an athletic scholarship. There are no limits on coaches contacting student-athletes from their freshman to junior years. Senior year, the same rules apply unless the student-athletes has enrolled in another institution. A NJCAA institution may pay for one visit to its campus for the student-athlete for two day and two nights, no longer, and only to the campus and community where campus is located. A NJCAA recruiter may purchase meals for their prospect, but only at the value provided to them by the college. In order to receive an official visit from a NJCAA college, a student-athlete must be a senior and have all credit requirements.

If basketball is your student-athlete's sport of choice, I hope the above information has been helpful to you in some way as well. Earlier I mentioned a National Letter of Intent. This is very important to know, as you may have heard of signing days for different sports and heard the term, letter of intent. A National Letter of Intent is just as it sounds, a letter that a student-athlete signs that shows they have intentions of attending the said institution in which they signed an agreement with.

Division I or Division II schools are the only ones that sign a National Letter of Intent under NCAA. Once a student-athlete signs NLI, they are agreeing to attend the college for at least one academic year and in return, the college is agreeing to give financial aid to student for one academic year. There are stipulations to this: the student has to be admitted to the school and be eligible for financial aid according to NCAA eligibility guidelines. Not signing a NLI has no bearing on financial aid assistance for a student-athlete when it comes to playing a sport, it is strictly a voluntary action. NJCAA athletes also sign a Letter of Intent to show commitment to an institution for one academic year.

Signing a National Letter of Intent on signing day can be very exciting for student-athletes as they are surrounded by coaches, parents, family and friends that have been there to support them along the way. Now, once a letter of intent is signed, the student-athlete is no longer marketable to any other school. They are off limits and the recruiting process for them has come to an end. If a student-athlete decides that he or she is not happy with the choice that has been made, they can ask for a release from the school in which a letter of intent was signed. The most important thing to know is that if your student-athlete signs a Letter of Intent with one school and decided to attend another school but did not get an official release, they will lose one full year of eligibility and will have to complete one full academic year at the new school before being eligible to compete in their sport.

The next section will discuss NCAA eligibility rules. As a parent, you listen to coaches, recruiters, other parents, family, and friends often taking what they say as truth because you just may not know or understand any of it. It is my hope that this information this has given you a better understanding of the recruiting process and that you are able to assist your student-athlete in achieving their athletic goals while keeping academics first.

Be Eligible

When it comes to being eligible for NCAA Division schools, it comes down to knowing the guidelines and doing what it takes from day one to make it happen. Once entering high school as a ninth grader, students become responsible for earning credits to graduate. This chapter is by far the most important, if you want to help your student-athlete successfully pursue an athletic career beyond high school. The topics discussed in this chapter all tie closely to each other and must be done by each student-athlete if they wish to play sports beyond high school at an NCAA Division school. The first topic is graduation requirements, what must be done in order to graduate from high school.

The NCAA requirements align with graduation requirements of most states around the country, but set a stricter pattern of courses that must be completed by a student-athlete's senior year. Let me explain. The graduation requirements discussed pertain to Georgia high schools only, and may vary depending on programs your students may be involved in, such as prep, magnet, etc. According to the general graduation requirements, in order to graduate from a high school in Georgia, a student must complete 23 credits. The 23 credits must come from the following areas; four credits in Language Arts, four credits in Mathematics, four credits in Science, three credits in Social Science, one credit for Physical Education and Health, three credits under a career pathway which includes World Language and Fine Arts, and lastly four credits in electives (non-core classes they can choose to take). Now, to look at the breakdown of these classes.

For Language Arts, a student will take 9th grade Literature and 10th grade Literature. When it comes to 11th and 12th grades, different schools do things in different order, but within the two years students may take American, World, British, and/or Multicultural Literature. Students may also be enrolled in AP course and even college courses during this time as well. Overall they must satisfy four Language Arts credits. In Mathematics, 9th grade students will take Algebra, 10th graders will take Geometry, 11th graders will take Advanced Algebra or Pre- Calculus, and 12th graders may take Pre-Calculus, Mathematics of Finance, Advanced Mathematical Decision Making, AP Calculus, AP Statistics, or College Calculus. Please keep in mind, this is a suggested course list and the actual courses may be named differently depending on the school and state.

With Science, students may take the courses in various orders, most likely a 9th grader will take Biology. When in 10th, 11th, and 12th grade, they may take Physical Science, Chemistry, Physics, Earth Science, Environmental Science, Human Anatomy and Physiology, AP Science Courses, or any identified Science CTE course. The order of courses will vary with each school district but these courses give you an idea. With Social Science, there are only three credits required. In Georgia, I have seen these courses also taken at various stages, depending on the county. The Social Science courses are World History, American History, Economics, and American Government. Some schools may also offer Geography as an elective. With core courses, it also depends on the course being a semester course or a yearlong course, which varies as well by county and/or school. Please always ask counselors for clarification. The above information is only to give you an idea of the course progression your student should be on.

For the one Health and Physical Education credit, students will take half in Personal Fitness and the other half in Health, or they may take three units of JROTC to satisfy the Personal Fitness credit. Most of the time, students love taking the Physical Education classes even if they are in JROTC. Students must complete three credits of Career Technology/Agricultural

Education, World Language, or Fine Arts classes. This can be done in any order as some students may enter high school with World Language credit. For the students who take two years of the same World Language in middle school, they may receive credit toward their high school requirements. It takes two years of the same World Language middle school course to equal one high school course credit. Lastly are the elective units that are required, each student must meet four of these for graduation. Elective classes are non-core classes that may be taken in an area of interest to the student, such as band, chorus, art, drama, etc. The elective courses are not counted as the Career Technology courses, this is in addition to those three required credits. Other electives may fall under Social Sciences such as Psychology and Sociology courses, or any other World Language course after the normally required two years for college prep track.

Please keep in mind that the above information is the minimum requirement for graduation in Georgia. There are exceptions and rules that apply to each county and each school and other states. Please always adhere to those rules and sit down with a counselor to ensure your student gets on and stays on the right path. Also remember that NCAA has an approved course list (48 H) for each school. The courses that your student takes should appear on this approved course list. All guidance counselors should be aware of this and most of the time, they align with graduation requirements, but there are some elective courses in areas that can be taken to help boost core grade point average.

Being eligible means having the grades and other requirements needed to play on a team in high school, and to receive athletic and academic scholarships in college. The NCAA (National Collegiate Athletic Association) is the governing body when it comes to setting rules and regulations with student-athletes obtaining athletic scholarships. They set high standards for student-athletes as education is a priority for them as well as athletics. They want to see student-athletes succeed in both areas. I will give you the NCAA Division I and Division II eligibility requirements that your student-athletes need to have to be eligible to receive an athletic scholarship and play their freshman year in college. Division III, NAIA, and NJCAA are different and I will touch on those as well. As of August 2016, the NCAA eligibility requirements are different from the past. For the player that could normally get into school and receive athletic aid with a 2.0, those days are no longer. Division I schools require student-athletes to meet academics standards for NCAA core courses and test scores.

For a student-athlete to be a **full qualifier** and be eligible to practice, compete, and receive an athletic scholarship being a full-time first year student-athlete, students must first graduate high school and meet certain requirements. Those requirements are to complete 16 core courses that have been NCAA approved. These courses will vary in name from school to school. Most of these 16 core courses align with your regular graduation standards and should be taken regardless. Of those 16 core required courses, 10 of them must be completed before the start of senior year (7th semester), and of those 10, seven of the courses must be in English, Math or Natural/Physical Science. Student-athletes need to keep in mind that once their senior year begins, any of those 10 courses may not be repeated to try to improve grade point average.

Another requirement is to have at least a 2.3 grade point average in core courses and earn scores on the SAT (combined score) or ACT (sum score) that aligns with core grade point average according to the Division 1 or Division 2 sliding scale. The sliding scale is used to balance your test scores and core course grade point average. If you have low test scores

(SAT or ACT), then you will need a higher GPA to be eligible. Likewise, if you have a low GPA, then you will need a higher test score to be eligible according to NCAA.

The 16 NCAA core courses must be in the following areas: four years of English; three years of Math (Algebra 1 or higher); two years of Natural/Physical Science (to include one lab if offered); two years of Social Science; one additional year of either English, math or Natural/Physical Science; and lastly four additional credits that can be taken in either English, Math, Natural/Physical Science, Social Science, Foreign Language, Comparative Religion or Philosophy. The above NCAA requirements align close with many high school graduation requirements. Keeping the numbers 16, 10, and 7 (**16** core courses, **10** before senior year, and **7** in certain courses) in mind is important and knowing the areas needed will ensure a student-athlete is on the right path to be eligible and complete requirements in the four years of high school.

Now if a student-athlete graduates high school on time and does indeed plan to attend a Division 1 school, they may complete just one additional NCAA core course within one year of graduating to help meet the core requirements or to help improve grade point average. The good thing about this consideration is that the core-course does not have to be

completed at student-athletes home school as long as a transcript can be

provided to receive the credit. How awesome is that as one last effort to

make the best of the grade point average. To receive an academic

certification, student-athletes must have an official transcript for all

schools attended, test scores, and be on a Division 1 schools' request list,

and there cannot be any open tasks academically.

Student-athletes who do not meet the requirements may still be eligible

to receive some athletic aid and practice in the initial year of enrollment if

certain other requirements are met. If enrolled in a Division 1 school and

requirements have not been met, student-athletes may not compete.

However, student-athletes may qualify as an **academic redshirt**, which

means they may practice during their first term in college and also receive

athletic aid, but they may not participate in any competition. There are a

different set of rules for an academic redshirt. A student-athlete must be

a graduate of a high school, complete the 16 core courses (that doesn't

change), but no grades are locked in so they have the opportunity to

repeat a course after the seventh semester (start of senior year), and it will be used for initial eligibility. For academic redshirt, student-athletes must also meet the test (ACT/SAT) score requirements according to sliding scale and have a minimum 2.0 grade point average. As mentioned previously, student-athletes must enter the code 9999 when they register to take the ACT or SAT in order for results to be sent to the NCAA eligibility center, which will be discussed shortly.

Division II schools have another set of eligibility requirements which will be changing in August 2018 as it relates to grade point average and test scores. The current (good until August 1, 2018) Division II requirements still require student-athletes to complete the 16 core courses: three years of English; two years of Mathematics (Algebra 1 or higher); two years of Natural/Physical Science (1 year of lab if available); three years of additional English, Mathematics or Natural/Physical Science; two years of Social Science; and four years of additional courses (from English, Mathematics, Natural/Physical Science, Social Science, Foreign Language or Comparative Religion/Philosophy). Student-athletes must graduate from high school with at least a 2.0 grade point average and SAT sum score of 820 (math and reading) or a sum score of 68 on ACT.

After August 1, 2018, Division II schools will require student-athletes to have the same 16 courses above completed, but the grade point average increases to 2.2 instead of 2.0 to be eligible. While the GPA increases, the scores for the SAT and ACT will be on a sliding scale. Both Division I and Division II scales can be found at the back of this book as a reference. You have heard the term core course several times, so keep in mind that a core course must be an academic, four-year college preparatory course in the following subjects: English; Math (Algebra 1 or higher); Natural or Physical Science; Social Science; Foreign Language; or Comparative Religion or Philosophy.

Core courses must be taught at or above a high school's regular academic level and a student must receive credit towards high school graduation and the course must appear on official transcript showing the title of the course, the grade received, and credit gained for the course. When it comes to taking courses in high school, often students want to take easier courses, but must keep in mind the core course requirements, and that not all courses are NCAA approved core courses. Most elective classes such as Fine Arts, Music, Business courses, Career Pathways courses, Physical Education courses, any type of Vocational course, or courses in which you receive credit just by taking a test, are not acceptable. There are situations where students fall behind in a course, it happens.

The main thing to remember here is that the course has to be made up according to the timeline for NCAA eligibility requirements. Also remember that credit recovery courses must also meet NCAA standards which are: there must be instructor-led interaction between teacher and student, and a time frame must be established for completion of the course; course must compare to regular course in length, rigor, and content; credit recovery policies must be followed according to school policy; the course must appear on transcript as a recovery credit; and lastly, the course must be on the NCAA approved course list.

Now that the grades have been made and you are wondering how it all calculates, this is where the NCAA Eligibility Center comes into play as they are the guiding source to make sure you are eligible. Registration with the NCAA Eligibility Center (also called Clearinghouse) is a must if a student-athlete wishes to play a sport at a Division 1 or Division II school. Student-athletes need to create an account their sophomore year of high school and will need to have an email address to do so. There is a cost for the NCAA Eligibility Center, but it can be waived if the student-athlete received a fee waiver for the SAT or ACT. This can be done by having the high school counselor submit fee waiver documentation once registration is completed.

The NCAA Eligibility Center calculates the course grade point average according to the grades that are earned in that course. The NCAA will only use the best grades for each required course, so in the case that you took a course over to improve the grade, the better grade will be used in calculation of your grade point average. Grades from additional core courses will only be used if they improve your grade point average. The core course grade point average is calculated on a 4.0 scale where numeric grades are changed to letter grades. Grades received that have a plus or minus are not used by the NCAA in calculation of your grade point average. When there is a pass or fail received for a core course, the NCAA will use the lowest passing grade for calculation. Weighted honors and advanced placement courses may help improve grade point average if the NCAA is notified of the weight by the school, otherwise it gets normal points like a regular class.

The calculation of the grade point average by the NCAA is done using quality points. A grade of an A equals 4 points, B equals 3 points, C equals

2 points, and a D equals 1 point. To determine quality points received for a course you multiply the quality points earned for the grade by the amount of credit earned from that course. For instance, a Chemistry course that is a semester (0.50 units) long in which a grade of an A (4 points) is received, the quality point received would be 2 (4 points x 0.50 units = 2.00 quality points. If you have the same course that is a yearlong with a grade of an A received, the quality points received would be 4 (4 points x 1.00 units = 4 quality points). A worksheet from a student that takes semester classes versus yearlong courses looks different because with semester classes different grades can be received each semester and cause the calculation to be different. However with yearlong courses, there is one grade at the end. Hopefully this information has given you more insight into how important grades are and why as a freshman in high school, your student-athlete needs to take each class seriously and make the best grades possible.

When registering with the NCAA Eligibility Center, student-athletes are asked questions about the sports they have participated in to determine their amateur status. Activities such as signing a contract with a professional team, playing with professionals, accepting payment or special treatment for playing a sport, having an agent or delaying full-time college enrollment to play in organized sports competitions are among the activities that may impact a student-athletes amateur status. If

enrolling at a Division I or Division II school for the fall semester, an amateurism certification can be requested on or after April 1, before enrollment. If enrolling in the spring, a request can be made on or after October 1, before enrollment.

Keep in mind that after graduation, a student-athlete has a certain amount of time, known as a "grace period", to enroll in a NCAA school. If a student-athletes does not enroll at the first chance following grace period, they lose one season of competition for each calendar year they continue to participate in organized competition. In most cases, full-time enrollment can be delayed for one year after graduating high school without impacting eligibility. Make sure you read all the rules according to NCAA about eligibility when making this decision. Of course, going straight to college from high school would be the ideal option for most, but things happen and a delay may need to occur for a student-athlete to get better prepared. Whatever the case may be, never give up, support your student-athlete from the start of 9th grade until they reach their collegiate academic and athletic goals.

Another important piece to eligibility has to do with the transfer rules. Often times, student-athletes will start at one institution and then want to transfer to another for various reasons, but the eligibility rules need to be understood completely when making these types of decisions. For Division I schools a student-athlete has five years of eligibility to play four years of competition, in which the clock starts the first semester a student enrolls full-time (12 units) and it is a continuous clock no matter what. By continuous, I mean that if a student-athlete spends any down time not playing in competition but still enrolled in academics, the clock is still ticking.

If the decision is made to red-shirt or to go part-time, the five years is still being counted against you. For Division II or III schools, there is a little more flexibility and student-athletes have 10 full-time semesters or 15 quarters to complete their four years of competition play if enrolled full-time. If enrolled as a full-time or part-time student, while competing for the school, a semester or quarter is being calculated and used. If student-athletes only attend part-time and do not compete or are not enrolled for a term, then no time is used. There are always exceptions to the rule in some way. Make sure you are knowledgeable for your exact situation. Transferring from one school to the next can be tricky, but before giving you some information on that, let us take a look at eligibility for Division III, Junior Colleges, and NAIA schools.

For Division III schools, each individual school sets their own rules and there is no need to register with NCAA Eligibility Center. Contacting the coach on specifics is the best way to see about qualifying for a Division III school, knowing that graduation from high school is the most important requirement. For a NJCAA school, to be able to compete, student-athletes must graduate from high school or have a GED. Student-athletes must also be enrolled full-time, 12 credit hours, by the 15th calendar day of the beginning of the regular term per academic calendar. With NAIA schools, they have their own eligibility center that student-athletes need to register on to determine status. The requirements are to graduate from high school with at least a 2.0 grade point average on a 4.0 scale and to earn an 18 on the ACT or an 860 on the SAT, with Critical Reading and Math sections.

When making the decision to attend college after high school, whether playing a sport or not, make sure research is done on a full scale as to what the school has to offer, qualifications and the guidelines once accepted. Once accepted to an institution, student-athletes may find that it is not the best fit for them and want to transfer, and there is nothing wrong with this whatsoever. Knowing the rules to transfer and being able to transfer with ease will help a lot. The rules for transferring are subject to change at any time and research must be done according to each individual situation to get the best results because you never want to put your student-athlete's education or eligibility in jeopardy.

As a student-athlete, it is best to always protect yourself and do your homework going in for each possible scenario so you do not get stuck. A few things to think about before considering a transfer are; which school is right for you both academically and athletically, know the rules of the school you wish to attend, understand that each division has its own set of rules; gain full knowledge of the admission requirements for the new school that you wish to attend, keep in mind the rules for contact in each situation; and the last thing to do once all has been found out would be to apply to the new school. The transfer rules change so make sure you do your own research. The following information is intended only to be a guide and give some basic knowledge. I will touch on one of the most common types of transfers, being from a Junior College to a NCAA institution. When attending a NJCAA (Junior College) school and wanting to transfer to a four-year institution, student-athletes must graduate with a 2.5 GPA in order to be a qualifier in a Division I school and compete. If a student-athlete has not graduated, they must have attended the two-year college as a full-time student for at least one semester, have 12 transferable degree credits for each semester attended along with a minimum 2.5 GPA, to be a Qualifier, possibly without competing. Students cannot use more than two units of PE courses to meet the transfer degree credit or GPA requirements.

There are so many different rules when it comes to transferring, so please make sure you are aware of the specific rules before getting started. The key to transferring is to always stay eligible, academically and athletically, by being on top of your classes and grades. Meeting the transfer credit hour requirements is very important for each institution type. Being told you have to sit out is common, but remember there are many exceptions to the rules, so **ALWAYS** do your research.

One last important piece to it all is financial aid. Regardless of eligibility status, each student and student-athlete alike must complete a FAFSA

(Free Application for Federal Student Aid) in order to be considered for

financial aid if certain qualifications are met. Federal Student Aid is a part

of the U.S. Department of Education, and provides grants, loans, and

work-study funds for college. The basic eligibility requirements include: be

able to demonstrate a financial need; be a citizen or an eligible noncitizen;

have a valid social security number; be registered with Selective Services

(males between ages 18 and 25); be enrolled or accepted as a student in a

degree or certificate program; be enrolled at least half-time to be eligible

for Direct Loan Program funds; maintain satisfactory academic progress;

sign the certification statement stating that you are not in default on a

federal student loan; and show that you are qualified to obtain a college

education having received a high school diploma or GED. There are

deadlines for applying for financial aid. The current year is normally open

from Jan of that year until June 30 of the next year. (EX: For the 2016-17

year, the application is available from January 1, 2016 until June 30,

2017). The rule of thumb with student-athletes is to have the FASFA

completed by as soon as possible after January 1 of the year to enroll in

college and definitely by March 1. Some programs are limited in funds and

it is always best to apply as soon as you can. There are deadlines as well

for state student aid, and this information can be found on the FASFA website. Schools may also offer different forms of aid and it is always best to check with the school of choice to get clarification.

When completing the financial aid form, always know which schools you want to have to receive your financial aid reward information, and be prepared to enter the school code in order for the information to be sent to the schools you choose. A student's dependency status determines whose information needs to be reported on FASFA. A dependent student must report personal information and the information of their parents. An independent student must report their own information and their spouse's, if married. The federal student aid programs are based on the idea that it is up to the student and the student's family to pay for their education. With dependent students, because they have the support of parents, the parent's information must be assessed as well. This is done in order to get a full picture of the family's financial abilities. There is so much information on the financial aid process and the forms that need to be completed. Please visit the website to ensure you get a full view of what it requires and how it works for your student. As stated several times, always do your own research. This information is to be used as a guide.

Character is Key

Abraham Lincoln stated, "Reputation is the shadow. Character is the tree." A person's character is how other people view them and becomes what people see as their reputation, whether good or bad. We live in a society where a person's character is very easily tarnished and once this is done, it can be very hard to regain a new image. Student-athletes are under more and more pressure with the added use of social media, which can make or break them when it comes to being recruited athletically for scholarships, because everyone is watching. As a parent, we always want what is best for our children, in school and in life as a whole. We can teach those values and instill in them what is right from wrong, but in any given instance, they may question what was taught. For this reason alone, we cannot give up or give in, we must stay in our children's' lives no matter what. As they get older, giving them a little leeway way is fine, but still know what is going on. Have those conversations that are uncomfortable, be on their social media pages, check their rooms, know who their friends are, meet the other parents, be involved from all aspects.

When a student-athlete is preparing for recruitment, things are exciting, schools are coming in to visit them, talking to them, they are going on visits, and it all becomes more than they could imagine. In this excitement, they want it to be known they are being recruited so they take to social media. Once something is put on social media, it gives others free reign to make comments on any given situation; this can be positive or negative. Student-athletes have to learn how to talk on social media, what is proper to say and not say, what is the proper way to respond to someone else, or even if a response is even warranted.

Not just with social media, but when it comes to meeting coaches face to face, there is a right and wrong way to go about it. For this section, I reached out to some of my closest coaching friends again, and it was all the same feedback. Athletes have to have manners, know how to use them, know how to speak to adults, and know how to react to conversations, especially conversations that can lead them to academic and athletic scholarships. There are things that get us all upset because we are human, there are also things that we want to exemplify when speaking to others, there are things we want our friends to know about us that may not always be known, such as places we may go or certain things we may be doing. All of this is fine, but for a student-athlete this can be very touchy and they have to remain sensible with each step they take when being recruited. When being recruited, young student-athletes have to carry on a different demeanor. They should not be so carefree or use social media as an outlet to just let it all out. Posting pictures of the opposite sex in a bad manner, partying, smoking or any bad behavior is not a smart move. Also responses to other social media postings can cause major problems as well. Student-athletes have to be able to think before they act and realize that once something is out there, there is no getting it back. Often times, actions are taken impulsively, not thinking about the consequence behind it. The world is cold and the smallest comment or picture can be taken out of context and lead down a path that is one-way and very hard to turn around.

Talking social media, there have been many instances where a student-athlete has had their scholarship taken away because of social media behavior. When coaches are interested in an athlete, they want to know the full person they are investing in. Coaches will follow student-athletes and sometimes parents on social media to help get the full scope of what is going on. One major misconception that student-athletes have is that because they are talented, they are irreplaceable and this is certainly not the case. Even if a National Letter of Intent has been signed, a coach can still rescind the offer due to behavior on social media. There have been several occasion where high school and college athletes have had their scholarships taken away because of inappropriate postings on twitter such as nudity, language, racial content, and posting about receiving benefits from various places that are considered a violation. All you have to do is google it and the situations are there, they are real, and this happens all the time. Speaking with Coach Craig Agee, Assistant/Wide Receiver Coach at Tuskegee University, he stated, "Student-athletes need to understand that coaches indeed follow them on social media and they need to be selective and private about who they follow, and who they allow to follow them." Coach Agee also discussed the fact that budget constraints often make coaches from smaller schools use social media as a means of recruiting to see how the prospects handle themselves. He has had to deal with this one on one and stated that he gives athletes time to clean it up if he sees something he doesn't like. I can say that he is one of the good guys, some student-athletes aren't given a second chance.

Student-athletes should be using social media as a forum to show who they are and what they have to offer a college that may be interested in them. Each post should exhibit behavior that will help them move forward in their aspirations to play at the collegiate level, no matter the sport. Recruiters and coaches should be able to look at your social media history and see what sets you apart from other athletes they have seen. Understanding that there are no perfect people, but there has to be some thought given to each thing posted on social media when it can make the difference between being able to fulfill a dream or not. Keeping in mind that social media bridges that gap between contact periods, even when a coach can't contact an athlete, they can still view their social media accounts. Nothing is safe; all things are up for scrutiny when posted for the world to see. It is very important for student-athletes to also understand that even if they have just a few followers and tweet or send something out, their followers have followers, and before you know it, thousands of people see information they were not supposed to see. It is always best to tread very lightly when using social media and **THINK** before posting.

When face to face with coaches, student-athletes need to make sure they are using their manners and always being honest. Student-athletes must learn to give that firm handshake, make eye contact, and make the coaches feel that their school is their number one choice. Student-athletes also should show the excitement in taking to the coaches because when coaches feel a lack of interest, they move on to the next prospect. One of the biggest mistakes a student-athlete who is being recruited can make is not being where they should be when coaches come to see them. If a coach can't trust you to be in class where you need to be, how can he trust that you will go to class with no supervision in college? Any student-athlete will show just how much they really want to get to the next level when it comes down to it. Doing the necessary research, knowing what the rules are, keeping your social media clean, and being prepared for that on the spot moment are all things that need to take place when it comes to being ready.

You've heard the comments from a DI football coach, a DII football coach, and now I will leave you with commentary from an interview with a NJCAA basketball coach. I sat down with Coach Bruce Capers, Head Coach at Gordon State College in Barnesville, GA, and this is what he had to say regarding social media and recruiting. "The first thing I do with a recruit of interest is review his social media sites for content, because this will tell me who they are and what they are about." This was very interesting because even at the junior college level, social media has a major impact on how the coaches decide who they truly want to offer. Another insightful comment made by Coach Capers was that the Athletic Directors and Presidents of schools also have access to social media sites and you just never know who is watching. The best advice that you can give to your student-athlete is to always keep it clean, be respectful at all times, think before they act, and always do things that you would be proud of them doing.

THANK YOU

I want to thank you very much for making an investment in your student-athletes' future. Thank you for supporting my vision and mission to help student-athletes and parents understand the importance of academics when it comes to student-athletes preparing to play a sport at the next level after high school. Thank you for taking the time to read this book and I hope that you will pass it on or purchase a copy for someone else you know. It is my heart's desire that each student-athlete from middle school on will obtain this information and put it to use, starting with academics. It is so important that our youth know what is going on, what it takes, and take ownership of their future. Please always support your student, but allow them to grow and make some mistakes. We all know that life's most important lesson come from making the mistakes and learning from them. Again, thank you so much for your time and good luck to you and your student-athletes. I would love to hear any and all success stories and hear about good grades and scholarships received. Please feel free to email me at knowingwhatittakes@gmail.com. Thank you. Be Blessed!!!!!!

Please find specific states' high school graduation requirements below. The requirements below are a reflection as of May 2016. Many show the basic requirements and local boards are allowed to add more.

Alabama: 24 credits

English	4 credits
Math	4 credits
Social Studies	4 credits
Science	4 credits
P.E./Health	1.5 credits
Career Preparedness	1 credit
CTE/Foreign/Language/Arts	3 credits
Electives	2.5 credits

Alaska: 22.5 credits

English	4 credits
Math	3 credits
Social Studies	4 credits
Science	3 credits
P.E./Health	1.5 credits
Electives	7 credits

Arizona: 22 credits

English	4 credits
Math	4 credits
Social Studies	3 credits
Science	3 credits
CTE/Voc. Ed/Fine Arts	1 credit
Electives	7 credits

Arkansas: 22 credits

English	4 credits
Math	4 credits
Social Studies	3 credits
Science	3 credits
P.E./Health	1 credit
Arts	.5 credit
Electives	6 credits
Other (Oral communication)	.5 credit

California: 13 credits (plus other coursework adopted by local boards)

English	3 credits
Math	2 credits
Social Studies	3 credits
Science	2 credits
Foreign Language/Arts	1 credit
P.E./Health	2 credits

Colorado: 24 credits (Denver Public Schools); others are determined by local boards

English	4 credits
Math	4 credits
Social Studies	3 credits
Science	3 credits
P.E./Health	1 credit
Electives	9 credits

Connecticut: 20 credits (changes to 25 credits with c/o 2020)

English	4 credits	4 credits
Math	3 credits	4 credits
Social Studies	3 credits	3.5 credits
Science	2 credits	3 credits
CTE/Foreign Language/Arts	1 credit	7 credits
P.E./Health		1.5 credits
Electives/Senior Capstone	7 credits	2 credits

Delaware: 24 credits

English	4 credits
Math	4 credits
Social Studies	3 credits
Science	3 credits
World Language	2 credits
P.E./Health	1.5 credits
Career Pathway	3 credits
Electives	3.5 credits

District of Columbia (DC): 24 credits

English	4 credits
Math	4 credits
Social Studies	4 credits
Science	4 credits
World Language	2 credits
P.E./Health	1.5 credits
Art/Music	1 credit
Electives	3.5 credits

Florida: 24 credits

English	4 credits
Math	4 credits
Social Studies	3 credits
Science	3 credits
Arts	1 credit
P.E./Health	1 credit
Electives	8 credits

Georgia: 23 credits (detailed in Academic Years)

English	4 credits
Math	4 credits
Social Studies	3 credits
Science	4 credits
P.E./Health	1 credit
CTAE/World Language/Arts	3 credits
Electives	4 credits

Hawaii: 24 credits

English	4 credits
Math	3 credits
Social Studies	4 credits
Science	3 credits
CTE/Fine Arts/World Language	2 credits
P.E./Health	1.5 credits
Personal Transition Plan	0.5 credit
Electives	6 credits

Idaho: 46 credits

English	9 credits
Math	6 credits
Social Studies	5 credits
Science	6 credits
Humanities	2 credits
Health	1 credit
Electives	17 credits

Illinois: 24 credits (Chicago Public Schools)

English	4 credits
Math	3 credits
Social Studies	3 credits
Science	3 credits
World Language	2 credits
CTE/Fine Arts	4 credits
P.E.	2 credits
Electives	3 credits

Indiana: 40 credits

English	8 credits
Math	4 credits
Social Studies	4 credits
Science	4 credits
P.E./Health & Wellness	3 credits
College/Career Pathway	6 credits
Flex Credit	5 credits
Electives	6 credits

Iowa: 23 credits (Des Moines Public Schools)

English	4 credits
Math	3 credits
Social Studies	3 credits
Science	3 credits
Fine Arts	1.5 credits
P.E.	1 credit
Electives	7.5 credits

Kansas: 21 credits

English	4 credits
Math	3 credits
Social Studies	3 credits
Science	3 credits
Fine Arts	1 credit
P.E./Health	1 credit
Electives	6 credits

Kentucky: 22 credits

English	4 credits
Math	3 credits
Social Studies	3 credits
Science	3 credits
Fine Arts	1 credit
P.E./Health	1 credit
Career	7 credits

Louisiana: 24 credits (LA Core 4 Track)

English	4 credits
Math	4 credits
Social Studies	4 credits
Science	4 credits
P.E./Health	2 credits
Arts/Foreign Language	3 credits
Electives	3 credits

Maine: 41 credits (Portland Public Schools)

English	8 credits
Math	6 credits
Social Studies	6 credits
Science	6 credits
P.E./Health	3 credits
Fine Arts	2 credits
Electives	10 credits

Maryland: 21 credits

English	4 credits
Math	3 credits
Social Studies	3 credits
Science	3 credits
P.E./Health	1 credit
Fine Arts	1 credit
CTE/Foreign Language	3 credits
Electives	3 credits

Massachusetts: 22 credits

English	4 credits
Math	4 credits
Social Studies	3 credits
Science	3 credits
Foreign Language	2 credits
Arts	1 credit
Electives	5 credits

Michigan: 18 credits

English	4 credits
Math	4 credits
Social Studies	3 credits
Science	3 credits
P.E./Health	1 credit
Arts	1 credit
CTE/Foreign Language	2 credits
Online learning experience	

Minnesota: 21.5 credits

English	4 credits
Math	3 credits
Social Studies	3.5 credits
Science	3 credits
Arts	1 credit
Electives	7 credits

Mississippi: 24 credits

English	4 credits
Math	4 credits
Social Studies	4 credits
Science	4 credits
Business/Technology	1 credit
P.E./Health	1 credit
Arts	1 credit
Electives	5 credits

Missouri: 24 credits

English	4 credits
Math	3 credits
Social Studies	3 credits
Science	3 credits
P.E./Health	1.5 credits
Fine/Practical Arts	2 credits
Electives	7.5 credits

Montana: 20 credits

English	4 credits
Math	2 credits
Social Studies	2 credits
Science	2 credits
P.E./Health	1 credit
CTE/Arts	2 credit
Electives	7 credits

Nebraska: 200 credits

English	40 credits
Math	30 credits
Social Studies	30 credits
Science	30 credits
Multicultural Studies	5 credits
Financial Skills	5 credits
Career Planning	5 credits
Electives	55 credits

Nevada: 22.5 credits

English	4 credits
Math	3 credits
Social Studies	3 credits
Science	2 credits
P.E./Health	2.5 credits
Computers	0.5 credit
Electives	7.5 credits

New Hampshire: 20 credits

English	4 credits
Math	3 credits
Social Studies	2.5 credits
Science	2 credits
P.E./Health	1.5 credits
Arts/Information Tech.	1 credit
Electives	6 credits

New Jersey: 120 credits

English	20 credits
Math	20 credits
Social Studies	20 credits
Science	20 credits
P.E./Health	20 credits
Career Tech./Arts	10 credits
World Language	10 credits
Electives	10 credits

New Mexico: 24.5 credits

English	4 credits
Math	4 credits
Social Studies	3.5 credits
Science	3 credits
P.E./Health	1.5 credits
Career/Workplace	1 credit
Electives	7.5 credits

New York: 44 credits

English	8 credits
Math	6 credits
Social Studies	8 credits
Science	6 credits
P.E./Health	5 credits
Foreign Language	2 credits
Arts	2 credits
Electives	7 credits

North Carolina: 22 credits

English	4 credits
Math	4 credits
Social Studies	4 credits
Science	3 credits
P.E./Health	1 credit
Electives	6 credits

North Dakota: 24 credits

English	4 credits
Math	3 credits
Social Studies	3 credits
Science	3 credits
CTE/Foreign Language	3 credits
P.E./Health	1 credit
Electives	7 credits

Ohio: 20+ credits (state minimum + Econ/Financial Literacy & Fine Arts)

English	4 credits
Math	4 credits
Social Studies	3 credits
Science	3 credits
P.E./Health	1 credit
Electives	5 credits

Oklahoma: 23 credits

English	4 credits
Math	3 credits
Social Studies	3 credits
Science	3 credits
Fine Arts	1 credit
CTE/Foreign Language	2 credits
Electives (1 must be concentration)	7 credits

Oregon: 24 credits

English	4 credits
Math	3 credits
Social Studies	3 credits
Science	3 credits
P.E./Health	2 credits
CTE/Foreign Language	3 credits
Electives	6 credits

Pennsylvania: 21 credits

English	4 credits
Math	3 credits
Social Studies	3 credits
Science	3 credits
Fine Arts	2 credits
P.E./Health	1 credit
Electives	5 credits

Rhode Island: 24 credits

English	4 credits
Math	4 credits
Social Studies	3 credits
Science	3 credits
Arts/Technology	1 credit
P.E./Health/ROTC	4 credits
Electives	5 credits

South Carolina: 24 credits

English	4 credits
Math	4 credits
Social Studies	3 credits
Science	3 credits
Foreign Language/CTE	2 credits
P.E./JROTC	1 credit
Electives	7 credits

South Dakota: 22 credits

English	4 credits
Math	3 credits
Social Studies	3 credits
Science	2 credits
P.E./Health/Personal Finance	1 credit
Arts	1 credit
Electives	8 credits

Tennessee: 22 credits

English	4 credits
Math	4 credits
Social Studies	3 credits
Science	3 credits
P.E./Health/Personal Finance	2 credits
Arts	1 credit
Foreign Language	2 credits
Electives	3 credits

Texas: 26 credits (22 credit on basic track)

English	4 credits
Math	4 credits
Social Studies	4 credits
Science	4 credits
P.E.	1 credit
Foreign Language/Fine Arts	3 credits
Electives/Speech	6 credits

Utah: 24 credits

English	4 credits
Math	3 credits
Social Studies	3 credits
Science	3 credits
P.E./Health	2 credits
Arts/CTE	3 credits
Electives	6 credits

Vermont: 24 credits

English	4 credits
Math	3 credits
Social Studies	3 credits
Science	3 credits
P.E./Health	2 credits
Fine Arts/Business Technology	2 credits
Foreign Language	2 credits
Electives	5 credits

Virginia: 22 credits

English	4 credits
Math	3 credits
Social Studies	3 credits
Science	3 credits
P.E./Health	2 credits
Arts/CTE/Foreign Language	2 credits
Econ/Personal Finance	1 credit
Electives	4 credits

Washington: 20 credits /24 credits (starting with c/o 2019)

English	4 credits	4 credits
Math	3 credits	3 credits
Social Studies	3 credits	3 credits
Science	2 credits	3 credits
P.E./Health	2 credits	2 credits
Arts/CTE/World Language	2 credits	5 credits
Electives	4 credits	4 credits

West Virginia: 24 credits

English	4 credits
Math	4 credits
Social Studies	4 credits
Science	3 credits
P.E./Health	2 credits
Fine Arts	1 credit
Foreign Language/CTE	4 credits
Electives	2 credits

Wisconsin: 22 credits (Milwaukee Public Schools)

English	4 credits
Math	3 credits
Social Studies	3 credits
Science	3 credits
P.E./Health	2 credits
Fine Arts	1 credit
Electives	6 credits

Wyoming: 27 credits (Laramie County School District 1)

English	4 credits
Math	4 credits
Social Studies	3 credits
Science	3 credits
P.E./Health	2 credits
Electives	11 credits

The graduation requirements listed here for each state show the minimum requirements in most cases, or the requirements for the district that is the largest in that state. Always do your own research as there may be state testing, community service, or other requirements needed to obtain a state recognized diploma.

References/Helpful Websites

The following websites were used in my research and are going to be vital in keeping up with information and with researching information pertaining to your specific situations. Feel free to reach out to me as well with any questions at knowingwhatittakes@gmail.com. There are other websites that can give you the same information. This is my suggested list.

www.ncaa.org (NCAA information)

www.eligibilitycenter.org (Student-Athletes registration)

www.njcaa.org (Junior College information)

www.naia.org (NAIA information)

www.act.org (ACT registration)

www.collegereadiness.collegeboard.org (SAT registration)

https://fafsa.ed.gov (FAFSA-Federal Student Aid)

http://www.kaptest.com/act (ACT Test Prep)

https://www.khanacademy.org/test-prep/sat (SAT Test Prep)

http://www.nacacnet.org/ (National Association for College Admission Counseling)

https://web3.ncaa.org/hsportal/exec/hsAction?hsActionSubmit=searchHighSchool (Link to 48 H form to check for approved courses in your school or another high school)

The following pages show examples of NCAA sliding scale, GPA worksheets for a qualified student and a non-qualified student. Also notice the statistical information. Be informed at every step of the process.

Sliding Scale for Division I beginning August 1, 2016

Core GPA	SAT	ACT
3.550 & above	400	37
3.525	410	38
3.500	420	39
3.475	430	40
3.450	440	41
3.425	450	41
3.400	460	42
3.375	470	42
3.350	480	43
3.325	490	44
3.300	500	44
3.275	510	45
3.250	520	46
3.225	530	46
3.200	540	47
3.175	550	47
3.150	560	48
3.125	570	49
3.100	580	49
3.075	590	50
3.050	600	50
3.025	610	51
3.000	620	52
2.975	630	52
2.950	640	53
2.925	650	53
2.900	660	54
2.875	670	55
2.850	680	56
2.825	690	56
2.800	700	57
2.775	710	58
2.750	720	59
2.725	730	60
2.700	740	61
2.675	750	61
2.650	760	62
2.625	770	63
2.600	780	64
2.575	790	65
2.550	800	66
2.525	810	67
2.500	820	68
2.475	830	69
2.450	840	70
2.425	850	70
2.400	860	71
2.375	870	72
2.350	880	73
2.325	890	74
2.300	900	75
2.299	910	76
2.275	910	76
2.250	920	77
2.225	930	78
2.200	940	79
2.175	950	80
2.150	960	81
2.125	970	82
2.100	980	83
2.075	990	84
2.050	1000	85
2.025	1010	86
2.000	1020	86

ACADEMIC REDSHIRT

Image courtesy of NCAA.com

This worksheet is provided to assist you in monitoring your progress in meeting NCAA initial-eligibility standards. The NCAA Eligibility Center will determine your academic status after you graduate. Remember to check your high school's list of NCAA-approved courses for the classes you have taken.
Use the following scale: A = 4 quality points; B = 3 quality points; C = 2 quality points; D = 1 quality point.

English (4 years required)

10/7	Course Title	Credit	X	Grade	=	Quality Points (multiply credit by grade)
✓	Example: English 9	.5		A		(.5 x 4) = 2
	Total English Units					Total Quality Points

Mathematics (3 years required)

10/7	Course Title	Credit	X	Grade	=	Quality Points (multiply credit by grade)
	Example: Algebra 1	1.0		B		(1.0 x 3) = 3
	Total Mathematics Units					Total Quality Points

Natural/physical science (2 years required)

10/7	Course Title	Credit	X	Grade	=	Quality Points (multiply credit by grade)
	Total Natural/Physical Science Units					Total Quality Points

Additional year in English, mathematics or natural/physical science (1 year required)

10/7	Course Title	Credit	X	Grade	=	Quality Points (multiply credit by grade)
	Total Additional Units					Total Quality Points

Social science (2 years required)

10/7	Course Title	Credit	X	Grade	=	Quality Points (multiply credit by grade)
	Total Social Science Units					Total Quality Points

Additional academic courses (4 years required)

10/7	Course Title	Credit	X	Grade	=	Quality Points (multiply credit by grade)
Total	Total Additional Academic Units					Total Quality Points
	Total Quality Points from each subject area / Total Credits = Core-Course GPA		/		=	
		Quality Points	/	Credits	=	Core-Course GPA

Core-Course GPA (16 required) Beginning August 1, 2016, 10 core courses must be completed before the seventh semester and seven of the 10 must be a combination of English, math or natural or physical science for competition purposes. Grades and credits may be earned at any time for academic redshirt purposes.

Image courtesy of NCAA.com

Qualifier

Division I Worksheet

English (4 Years required)

Course	Credit	Grade	Points	Quality Points	
9th Grade	1	C	2	2	
10th Grade	1	C	2	2	
11th Grade	1	A	4	4	
12th Grade	1	B	3	3	
				0	
				0	
				0	
				0	
Total English Units	4			11	Total Quality Points

Mathematics (3 years required)

Course	Credit	Grade	Points	Quality Points	
Algebra	1	C	2	2	
Geometry	1	C	2	2	
Algebra II	1	B	3	3	
				0	
				0	
				0	
Total Mathematics Units	3			7	Total Quality Points

Natural/Physical Science (2 years required)

Course	Credit	Grade	Points	Quality Points	
Enviornmental	1	B	3	3	
Physical Science	1	A	3	4	
				0	
				0	
Total Natural/Physical Science Units	2			7	Total Quality Points

Additional Year in English, Mathematics or Natural/Physical Science (1 year required)

Course	Credit	Grade	Points	Quality Points	
Forensic Science	1	C	2	2	
				0	
Total Additional Units	1			2	Total Quality Points

Social Science (2 years required)

Course	Credit	Grade	Points	Quality Points	
American Government	1	C	2	2	
US History	1	A	4	4	
Total Social Science Units	2			6	Total Quality Points

Additional Academic Courses (4 Years required)

Course	Credit	Grade	Points	Quality Points	
Spanish 1	1	C	2	2	
Spanish 1	1	B	3	3	
Psychology	1	B	3	3	
Chemistry	1	B	3	3	
				0	
				0	
				0	
Total Additional Academic Units	4			11	Total Quality Points

Total Quality Points	Total Number of Credits	Core Course GPA
44	16	2.750

Example of a student who does qualify per NCAA requirements.

128

Division I Worksheet

English (4 Years required)

Course	Credit	Grade	Points	Quality Points	
9th Grade	1	C	2	2	
10th Grade	1	C	2	2	
11th Grade	1	D	1	1	
12th Grade	1	C	2	2	
				0	
				0	
				0	
				0	
Total English Units	**4**			**7**	**Total Quality Points**

Mathematics (3 years required)

Course	Credit	Grade	Points	Quality Points	
Algebra	1	C	2	2	
Geometry	1	D	1	1	
Algebra II	1	B	3	3	
				0	
				0	
				0	
Total Mathematics Units	**3**			**6**	**Total Quality Points**

Natural/Physical Science (2 years required)

Course	Credit	Grade	Points	Quality Points	
Enviornmental	1	D	1	1	
Physical Science	1	C	2	2	
				0	
				0	
Total Natural/Physical Science Units	**2**			**3**	**Total Quality Points**

Additional Year in English, Mathematics or Natural/Physical Science (1 year required)

Course	Credit	Grade	Points	Quality Points	
Forensic Science	1	D	1	1	
				0	
Total Additional Units	**1**			**1**	**Total Quality Points**

Social Science (2 years required)

Course	Credit	Grade	Points	Quality Points	
American Government	1	C	2	2	
US History	1	B	3	3	
Total Social Science Units	**2**			**5**	**Total Quality Points**

Additional Academic Courses (4 Years required)

Course	Credit	Grade	Points	Quality Points	
Spanish 1	1	D	1	1	
Spanish 1	1	B	3	3	
Psychology	1	B	3	3	
Chemistry	1	C	2	2	
				0	
				0	
				0	
Total Additional Academic Units	**4**			**9**	**Total Quality Points**

Total Quality Points	Total Number of Credits	Core Course GPA
31	16	1.938

Example of a student who does not qualify per NCAA requirements.

Division II Competition Sliding Scale

Use for Division II beginning August 1, 2018

Core GPA	SAT Verbal + Math ONLY	ACT
3.300 & above	400	37
3.275	410	38
3.250	420	39
3.225	430	40
3.200	440	41
3.175	450	41
3.150	460	42
3.125	470	42
3.100	480	43
3.075	490	44
3.050	500	44
3.025	510	45
3.000	520	46
2.975	530	46
2.950	540	47
2.925	550	47
2.900	560	48
2.875	570	49
2.850	580	49
2.825	590	50
2.800	600	50
2.775	610	51
2.750	620	52
2.725	630	52
2.700	640	53
2.675	650	53
2.650	660	54
2.625	670	55
2.600	680	56
2.575	690	56
2.550	700	57
2.525	710	58
2.500	720	59
2.475	730	60
2.450	740	61
2.425	750	61
2.400	760	62
2.375	770	63
2.350	780	64
2.325	790	65
2.300	800	66
2.275	810	67
2.250	820	68
2.225	830	69
2.200	840 & above	70 & above

Division II Partial Qualifier Sliding Scale

Use for Division II beginning August 1, 2018

Core GPA	SAT Verbal + Math ONLY	ACT
3.050 & above	400	37
3.025	410	38
3.000	420	39
2.975	430	40
2.950	440	41
2.925	450	41
2.900	460	42
2.875	470	42
2.850	480	43
2.825	490	44
2.800	500	44
2.775	510	45
2.750	520	46
2.725	530	46
2.700	540	47
2.675	550	47
2.650	560	48
2.625	570	49
2.600	580	49
2.575	590	50
2.550	600	50
2.525	610	51
2.500	620	52
2.475	630	52
2.450	640	53
2.425	650	53
2.400	660	54
2.375	670	55
2.350	680	56
2.325	690	56
2.300	700	57
2.275	710	58
2.250	720	59
2.225	730	60
2.200	740	61
2.175	750	61
2.150	760	62
2.125	770	63
2.100	780	64
2.075	790	65
2.050	800	66
2.025	810	67
2.000	820 & above	68 & above

Image courtesy of NCAA.com

This worksheet is provided to assist you in monitoring your progress in meeting NCAA initial-eligibility standards. The NCAA Eligibility Center will determine your academic status after you graduate. Remember to check your high school's list of NCAA-approved courses for the classes you have taken.

Use the following scale: A = 4 quality points; B = 3 quality points; C = 2 quality points; D = 1 quality point.

English (3 years required)

Course Title	Credit	X	Grade	=	Quality Points (multiply credit by grade)
Example: English 9	.5		A		(.5 x 4) = 2
Total English Units					Total Quality Points

Mathematics (2 years required)

Course Title	Credit	X	Grade	=	Quality Points (multiply credit by grade)
Example: Algebra 1	1.0		B		(1.0 x 3) = 3
Total Mathematics Units					Total Quality Points

Natural/physical science (2 years required)

Course Title	Credit	X	Grade	=	Quality Points (multiply credit by grade)
Total Natural/Physical Science Units					Total Quality Points

Additional years in English, math or natural/physical science (3 years required)

Course Title	Credit	X	Grade	=	Quality Points (multiply credit by grade)
Total Additional Units					Total Quality Points

Social science (2 years required)

Course Title	Credit	X	Grade	=	Quality Points (multiply credit by grade)
Total Social Science Units					Total Quality Points

Additional academic courses (4 years required)

Course Title	Credit	X	Grade	=	Quality Points (multiply credit by grade)
Total Additional Academic Units					Total Quality Points
Total Quality Points from each subject area / Total Credits = Core-Course GPA		/		=	
	Quality Points	/	Credits	=	Core-Course GPA

Image courtesy of NCAA.com

ODDS OF MAKING IT IN THE NFL

H.S. Football Players	1,086,627	Invited to Combine	350	
H.S. Football Seniors	310,465	Players drafted by NFL	256	
NCAA Football Players	70,147	Rookies making a Team	300	
NCAA FR Playing FB	20,042	% of players NCAA to NFL	1.6%	
% of HS players to NCAA	6.5%	NFL players reaching YR 4	150	
NCAA SRs playing FB	15,588	2014 NFL Min Salary	$420,000	
Players scouted by NFL	6,500	Income after Taxes (est.)	$252,000	

If your lucky enough to be one of the **6.5%** to become a NCAA football player, and one of the **1.5%** of that group to make it to the NFL, you'll be lucky to get **THREE** years out of it. At a minimum salary, you wont make enough to live on for the rest of your life. WHAT'S GOING TO PROVIDE FOR YOU AND YOUR FAMILY AFTER FOOTBALL IS OVER?

YOUR COLLEGE EDUCATION!

Image courtesy of Google Images; origination unknown

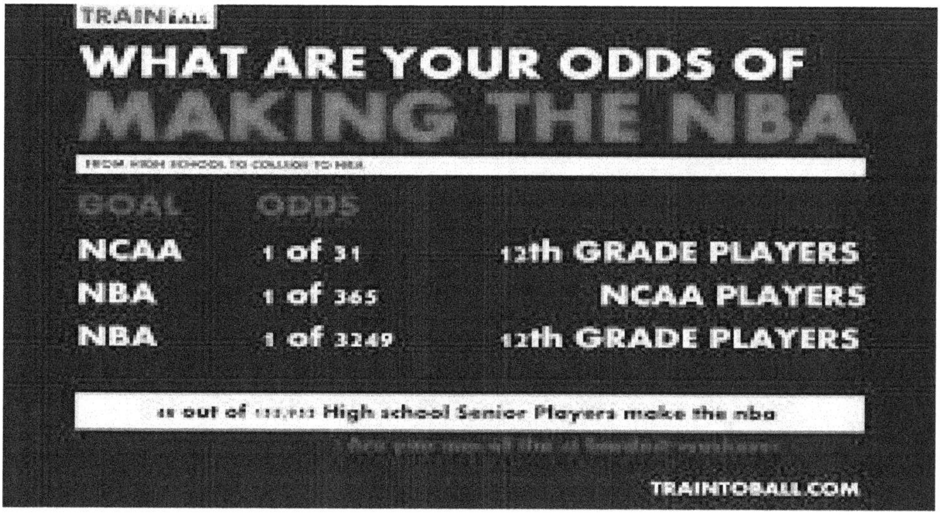

Image courtesy of Google Images; Traintoball.com